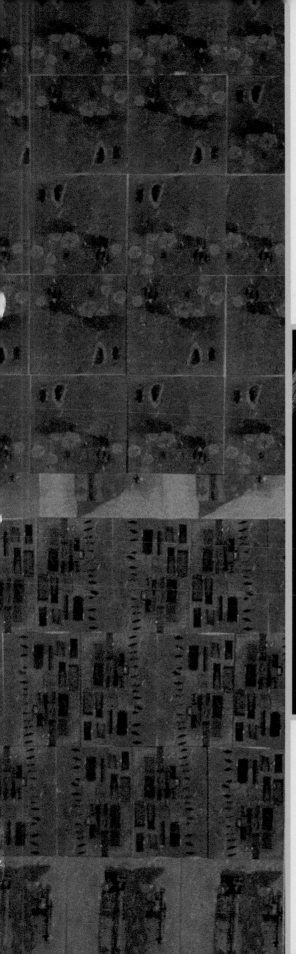

Fabulous Fabrics
Elegant & Innovative Techniques
to Embellish Textiles

Fabulous Fabrics

Elegant & Innovative Techniques
to Embellish Textiles

Mary Jo Hiney

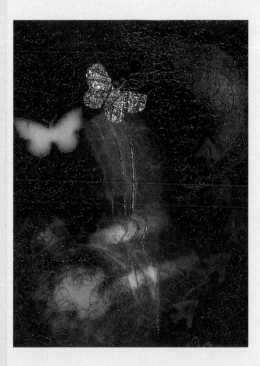

Sterling Publishing Co, Inc., New York
A Sterling/Chapelle Book

Chapelle Ltd.

Owner: Jo Packham

Editor: Linda Orton

Staff: Marie Barber, Ann Bear, Areta Bingham, Kass Burchett, Rebecca Christensen, Marilyn Goff, Holly Hollingsworth, Susan Jorgensen, Barbara Milburn, Karmen Quinney, Leslie Ridenour, Cindy Stoeckl, Gina Swapp

Photography: Kevin Dilley, photographer for Hazen Photography

Acknowledgements: Special thanks to the following manufacturers for their outstanding and innovative products: **Plaid** *for fabric paints,* **Mill Hill** *for beads,* **Silkpaint Corporation** *for fabric remover,* **Kreinik** *for metallic threads, and* **Blueprints-Printables** *for blueprint fabric.*

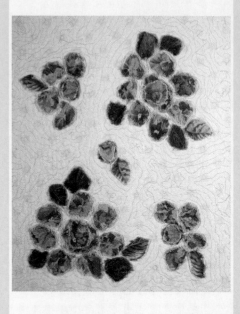

Page 1: Floorcloth by Jennifer Schumow and Mary Smull
Page 2: "Reaching" by Suzanne Evenson
Page 3: "Dreaming in the Garden IV" by Suzanne Evenson
Page 4: "Frayed Flower Appliqué" by Mary Jo Hiney,
*   Stenciled Scarf by Jane Dunnewold*

Library of Congress Cataloging-in-Publication

Hiney, Mary Jo.
  Fabulous Fabrics : elegant & innovative techniques to embellish textiles / Mary Jo Hiney.
    p. cm.
  "A Sterling/Chapelle Book."
  ISBN 0-8069-1909-4
    1. Fancy work. 2. Beadwork. 3. Embroidery. I. Title.

TT750 .H58 2000
746--dc21   99-087164

10 9 8 7 6 5 4 3 2 1

A Sterling/Chapelle Book

Published by Sterling Publishing Company, Inc.
387 Park Avenue South, New York, NY 10016
© 2000 by Chapelle Ltd.
Distributed in Canada by Sterling Publishing
% Canadian Manda Group, One Atlantic Avenue, Suite 105
Toronto, Ontario, Canada M6K 3E7
Distributed in Great Britain and Europe by Cassell PLC
Wellington House, 125 Strand, London WC2R 0BB, England
Distributed in Australia by Capricorn Link (Australia) Pty Ltd.
P.O. Box 6651, Baulkham Hills, Business Centre, NSW 2153, Australia
Printed in China
All Rights Reserved

Sterling ISBN 0-8069-1909-4

If you have any questions or comments, please contact:

Chapelle Ltd., Inc.
P.O. Box 9252
Ogden, UT 84409

Phone: (801) 621-2777
FAX: (801) 621-2788
e-mail: chapelle@chapelleltd.com

Mary Jo Hiney has avidly and continuously worked in a fabric-related field for the past twenty-four years, and hopes to continue for the next twenty-four years! One of Mary Jo's greatest loves is that of fabric and sewing. Just as when she was a child, she finds great joy in visiting a classic fabric store to explore the many glorious bolts of fabrics that are there.

Mary Jo is the author of *Beautiful Foundation-Pieced Quilt Blocks, Creating with Lace, Decorative Fabric Covered Boxes, Ribbon Basics, Romantic Fabric Covered Boxes, Romantic Silk Ribbon Keepsakes, Two-Hour Vests,* and *Victorian Ribbon and Lacecraft Designs.*

As with all projects of this nature, no one really works alone. Mary Jo would like to extend her gratitude to her friends at Chapelle for their steadfast support, especially Cindy Stoeckl for her daily encouragement and vital information, and Linda Orton for her beautiful presentations and skillful editing abilities.

This book is dedicated to the
Gift of Creative Spirit,
which brings about healing
and causes the light
to shine through simple
purpose of beauty.

A special and heartfelt thanks to such talented artists Karren K. Brito, Sandra Clark, Diana Contine, Suzanne Evensen, Roberta Glidden, Diane Lewis, Martha Matthews, Karen Perrine, Jennifer Schumow, Bobby Smead of Bernina, Mary Smull, and Laura Wasilowski, who took the time to send their artwork and photos for the gallery. The incredible skill and mastery they show through their art is truly an inspiration.

Table of Contents

"Farm" (detail)
Hand-dyed, Appliquéd, and
Quilted
Laura Wasilowski

"Pear Series No. 14"
Machine Embroidery
Martha Matthews

Untitled Yardage
Embellished Fabric
Jane Dunnewold

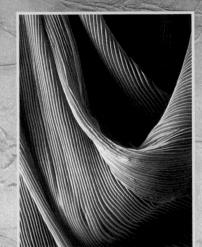

Shawl (detail)
Shibori
Karren K. Brito

Necklaces
Bead Embroidery
Karen Perrine

Shawl
Stamped
Diane Lewis

Introduction

The various techniques of decorating fabrics as expression of art have created a unique niche in the world of art. Fabric design and embellishment adds a personal touch to fabric as well as being an art form. Surface decoration may take the order of wearable or decorative art. The ways to adorn fabric are innumerable. In *Fabulous Fabrics*, techniques and ideas have been included, ranging from beading and stitchery to painting and dyeing. The included Gallery exhibits pieces done by acclaimed artists who make their living from embellishing fabrics and transforming them into works of art.

Fabrics invite us to touch and feel because of their corporeal nature. Embellished fabrics not only please the tactile senses, but they are visually appealing.

Draw a picture, using your sewing machine and thread for your art tools. Dye or paint the fabric surface and add

8

beadwork for accents. The number of ways to combine embellishment techniques are infinite.

Silk is a beautiful and perfect fabric to embellish with paint, pleats, or color discharge. Once the surface has been transformed, the silk itself becomes the perfect accent in scarves, shawls, or vests.

Create one-of-a-kind fabrics for decorative and functional use in the home, such as floor-cloths, pillows, and curtains.

The basic techniques are provided with complete instructions and material lists. Techniques may be used to cover one repeat or multiple repeats. The yardage with multiple

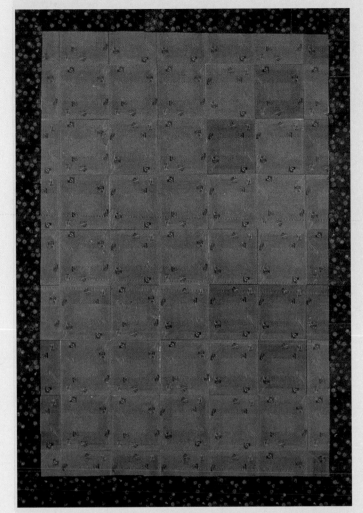

Floorcloth
Heat Transfer
Jennifer Schumow and Mary Smull

"Home"
Appliqué and Machine-quilted
Laura Wasilowski

repeats can be transformed into wearable art or for home decorating .

The Gallery art is made by artists who have mastered the various techniques and in many cases combined multiple techniques to create truly beautiful pieces of art. With some knowledge and practice, you can create fabrics that are truly masterpieces in every sense of the word.

Stitches and Flowers—

—Hand-stitching and Embroidery

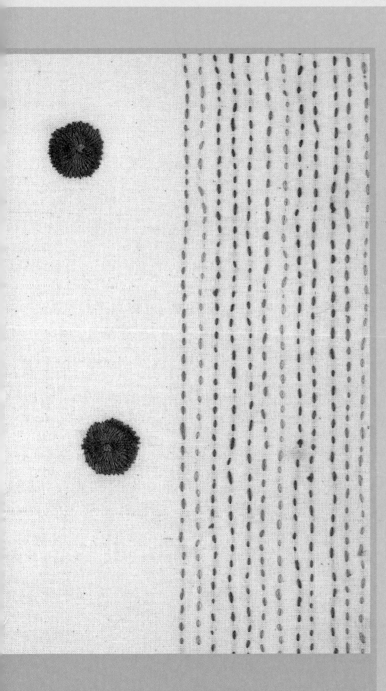

Materials:
Cotton fabric
Embroidery floss

Basic Tools:
Embroidery hoop
Embroidery needle: #5
Removable fabric marker
Ruler

Instructions

one Using marker and ruler, draw straight lines ¼" apart on ends of fabric. Mark center for flowers, approximately 4" apart.

two Using embroidery hoop, embroidery needle, and two strands of floss, sew running stitch along straight line. Alternate floss color in each line.

three Stitch French knot on flower mark. Vary the color of the French knot from flower to flower.

four Satin-stitch ¼"-long stitches around French knot like wagon wheel spokes. Satin-stitch second row of stitches between stitches of first row to complete flowers.

Fabric Care: Hand wash in cold water and line dry.

Running Stitch

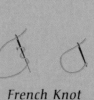

French Knot

Satin Stitch

Circles and Tucks—
—Embroidery and Tucks

Materials:
Embroidery floss: contrasting color
Raw silk fabric
Sewing thread

Basic Tools:
Circle template with various sizes
Embroidery needle
Iron and ironing board
Removable fabric marker: fine-tip,
    coordinating color
Sewing machine

Instructions

one Machine-stitch ⅛"-deep tucks
vertically, approximately 1" apart.
Using iron, press tucks in place.

two Using circle template and
fabric marker, trace circles in various
sizes onto tucked fabric.

three Using embroidery needle
and floss, stitch with running stitch
over traced circles. *Notes: Randomly
stitch circles, varying number of
strands, using one, three, or six strands.
Stitch some stitches going in same
direction as tuck, and others going in
opposite direction of tucks.*

Fabric Care: Hand wash in
cold water and lay flat to dry.

*Jacket
Row-stitched Fabric*

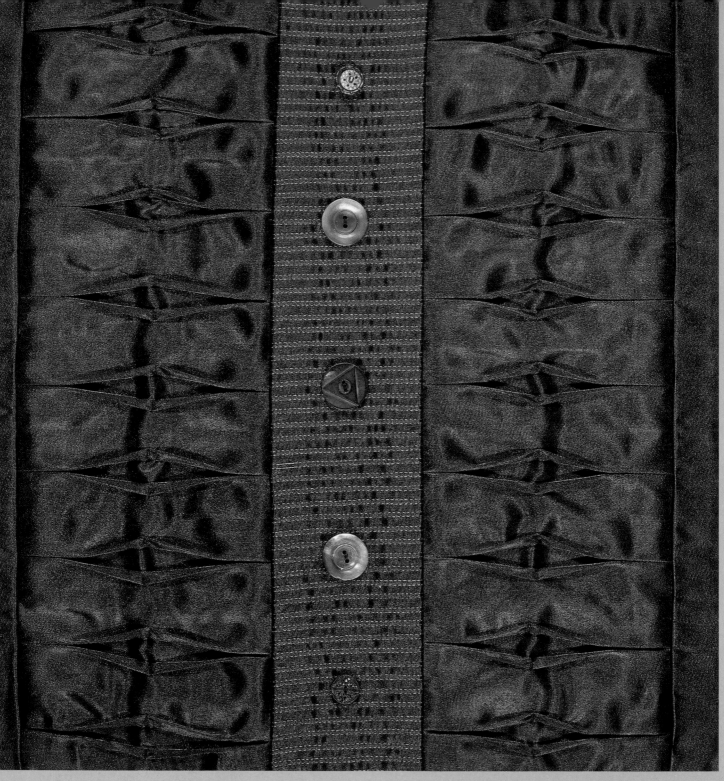

Pleats and Tucks—
—Machine-stitched Pleats and Tucks

Inverted box pleats with tucks give an elegant and tailored look to fabric. Accent the pleats and tucks with pintucks and vintage buttons.

The fabric for the box pleats was cut in a 6" width with the tuck being sewn in the middle. If you choose to make the inverted box pleats longer than 6", it would be advisable to plan tucks approximately every 3".

Fabric-folding does not have to be limited to pleats and tucks. Try folding fabric into paper origami shapes for unusual and unique forms that can be appliquéd onto fabric.

Materials:

Buttons: ½"–1", variety
Satin organdy fabric
Sewing threads: two colors

Basic Tools:

Iron and ironing board
Removable fabric marker: fine-tip
Ruler
Sewing machine with pintuck foot and double needle
Sewing needle
Straight pins

Instructions

Inverted Box Pleats and Tucks:

one Determine desired finished length and width, allowing 3¼" of fabric for each pleat. Unfinished fabric length is determined by doubling the finished size and adding 3".

two Using fabric marker and ruler, mark back side of satin organdy, beginning 1½" from edge in to 1⅝"-wide sections. Draw lines as shown in Diagram A.

three Fold solid line right to meet dashed line. Using iron and pins, press and pin in place. Fold next solid line left to meet dashed line, finger-press and pin. Repeat for remaining sections, leaving 1½" at end.

four Turn fabric over to right side. Fold first pleat center edge back ¼". Using needle and thread, tack in place. Repeat with next pleat edge, completing first inverted box-pleat section. Repeat with remaining sections.

Pintucks:

one Using sewing machine, pintuck foot, double needle, and two colors of thread, sew pintucks ⅛" apart across fabric. *Note: Refer to and follow your model sewing machine instructions for pintucks.*

two Using sewing machine and standard foot, sew inverted box-pleat sections to pintuck section with ⅝" seam and right sides together.

three Using needle and doubled thread, sew buttons to center of pintucked fabric.

Fabric Care: Dry clean.

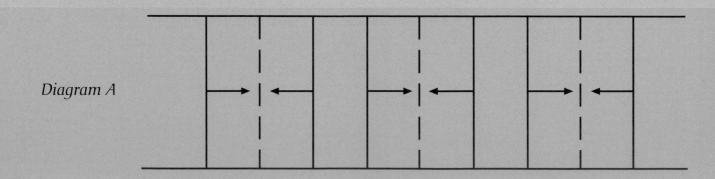

Diagram A

Quilted Vine—
—Free-motion Stitching

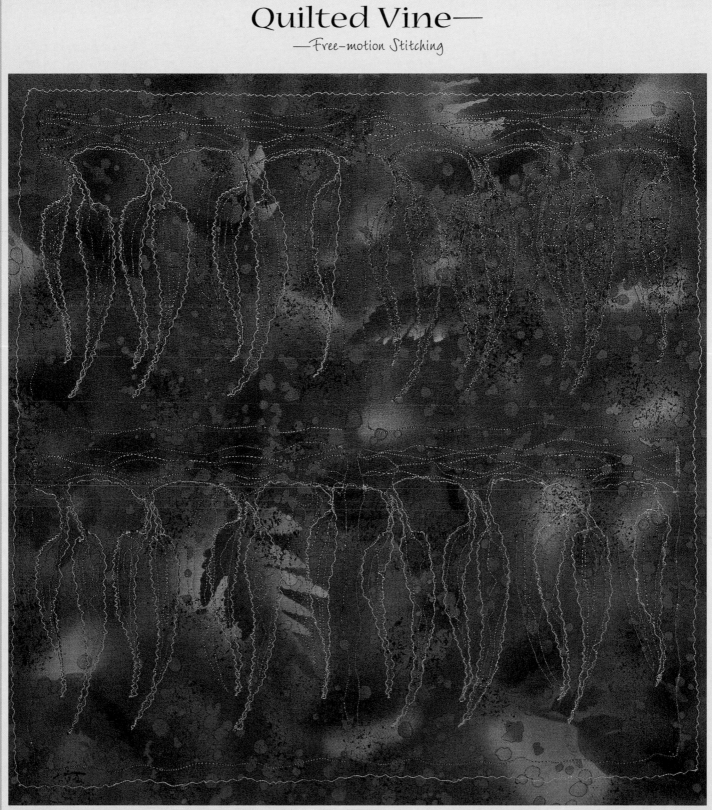

Fabric embellished by Mary Jo Hiney

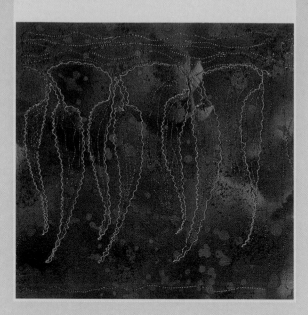

Free-motion stitching is a sewing machine technique, allowing random stitch movement by lowering a sewing machine's feed dogs. It is not necessary to have a top-of-the-line sewing machine in order to accomplish this. The darning foot attachment is used for free-motion stitching, since it sits slightly above the fabric surface when the foot is lowered and allows easy movement of the fabric. The sewing machine is ordinarily set on a basic straight stitch, but other basic utilitarian stitches may be used as well. Instead of clipping threads at the end of the design, backstitch along previous stitching to the next position and begin free-motion stitching.

Materials Per Repeat:

Cotton batting: lightweight
Fabrics:
    Cotton print
    Muslin
Threads:
    Machine-embroidery: two colors
    Sewing

Basic Tools:

Light box or glass placed over light
    source
Removable fabric marker: fine-tip
Sewing machine with darning foot
Sewing needle

Instructions:

one Do not preshrink fabrics. Enlarge Vine Pattern 168% on page 19 and photocopy. Place fabric and pattern over light box and using fabric marker, transfer pattern onto fabric. Repeat design as desired.

two Sandwich batting between wrong sides of cotton print and muslin. Using needle and sewing thread, baste layers together.

three Using sewing machine and darning foot, free-motion stitch design through layers with one color machine-embroidery thread. Fill in design areas with randomly guided stitches. *Note: Refer to and follow your model sewing machine instructions for free-motion stitching.*

four Outline the dominant leaf motifs with second color machine-embroidery thread and narrow, free-motion wave stitch.

five Machine wash quilted fabric in hot water and machine dry to pucker design.

Fabric Care: Machine wash in warm water and machine dry.

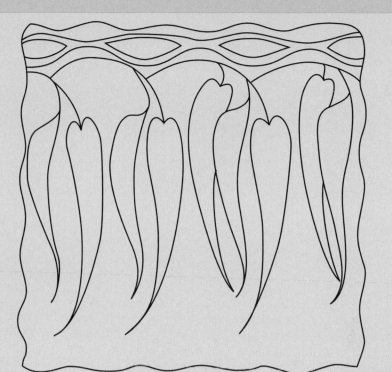

Note: The design also may be traced onto tissue paper or tear-away stabilizer. Place tissue paper onto sandwiched fabric, and pin in place. Free-motion stitch the basic design outline with one color. Tear tissue away and continue filling in design.

Vine Pattern
Enlarge 168%
Repeat Size 6¾" x 6¾"

Laura Wasilowski is a contemporary quilt maker and a creator of hand-dyed fabrics and threads. She has an undergraduate degree in costuming from the College of St. Benedict, and a Master of Art degree in Fiber from Northern Illinois University.

She is published in *The Art Quilt, Machine Quilting with Decorative Threads, Dyes and Paints, Color: The Quilter's Guide, New Quilts from Old Favorites, Visions "96"*, and *Quilt National: Contemporary Designs in Fabric*. Her works have been in many exhibits throughout the United States.

Laura's work revolves around a collection of vivid, hand-dyed fabrics that have been silk-screened, painted, or dyed. The colorful fabrics provide her inspiration for creating art quilts as well as the stories from family, friends, and home.

"Gardening Tip #2: Rest Often"
Appliqué and Machine-quilted
Laura Wasilowski

Cobwebbed Fabric—
—Free-motion Stitching

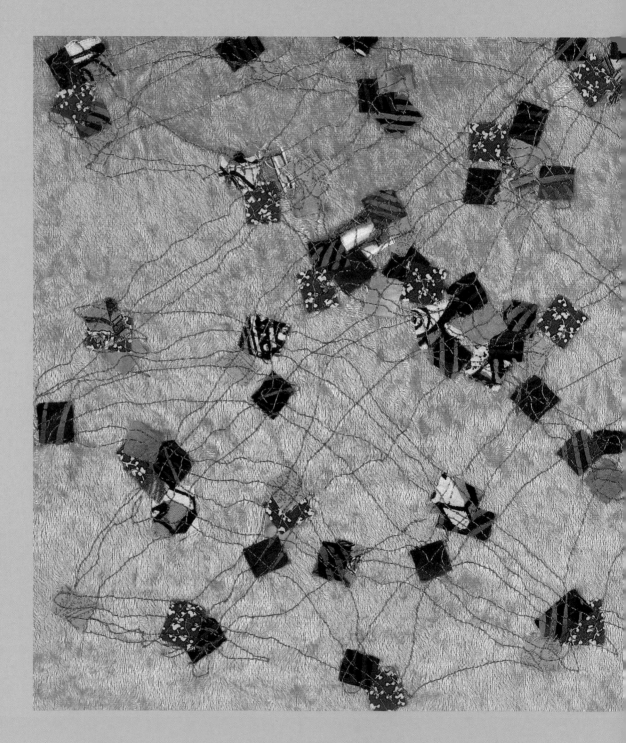

Materials:

Fabrics:
    Cotton print scraps
    Panne velvet
Machine-embroidery thread
Water-soluble stabilizer (same size as velvet)

Basic Tools:

Fabric scissors
Sewing machine with darning foot
Straight pins

Instructions:

Using fabric scissors, cut cotton scraps into small square and rectangular pieces. *Note: Straight cuts for squares and rectangles can be made quickly and efficiently by using a rotary cutter, ruler, and cutting mat.*

Arrange cotton pieces on right side of velvet. Place stabilizer over velvet and cotton pieces. Using straight pins, pin stabilizer to velvet and cotton pieces.

See Free-motion Stitching on page 18. Using sewing machine and darning foot, drop feed dogs and free-motion stitch diagonally several times over fabric scraps, moving to each grouping of cotton pieces until all pieces have been attached.

Soak fabric in cold water for five to ten minutes to dissolve stabilizer. Rinse fabric and allow to dry.

Fabric Care: Machine wash in warm water and machine dry.

Fabric embellished by Mary Jo Hiney

Shisha and Ribbon Quilt Squares—

—Easy Shisha Rings

Each repeat has eight 5" blocks, with shisha mirrors placed as desired. The assorted selection of braids and trims allows for variety. Combining metallics and black gives a richness and elegance to the velvet fabric.

Trim around the first eight-block repeat with fancy ribbons of varied widths.

Materials for 4 Blocks:

Embroidery floss: metallic
Fabric:
    Suede: black, min. of ¼ yd.
    Velvet print: 6"-squares (2), black/metallic
Metallic cord: fine, gold
Plastic rings: ¾" (10)
Ribbons and trims:
    ¼"-wide: 6", two varieties (1)
    ⅜"-wide: 6", two varieties (1)
    ¾"-wide: 6"
    ⅞"-wide: 6"
    1"-wide: 6"
    1½"-wide: 6", one variety (3)
            6", one variety (1)
    3"-wide: 6"
Sequins: copper, gold
Shisha mirrors: ½" (10)
Thread: black

Basic Tools:

Fabric glue
Fabric scissors
Needles:
    Chenille: #3
    Embroidery: #3
Pencil
Ruler
Sewing machine with darning foot
Straight pins

Instructions

Shisha Rings

Plain Shisha Ring:

one Using four 27" strands of embroidery floss, tie floss around plastic ring with double knot, leaving 3" tail. Using chenille needle, thread on long end of floss. Use buttonhole stitch to wrap ring as shown in Diagram A.

two When ring is completely covered, slide needle through first stitch to underside of ring. Slide needle through several more stitches and using fabric scissors, trim off remaining tail. Thread beginning tail and slide needle through last stitch to underside of ring. Slide needle through several more stitches and trim off remaining tail. *Note: Embroidered Shisha rings and mirrors can be purchased.*

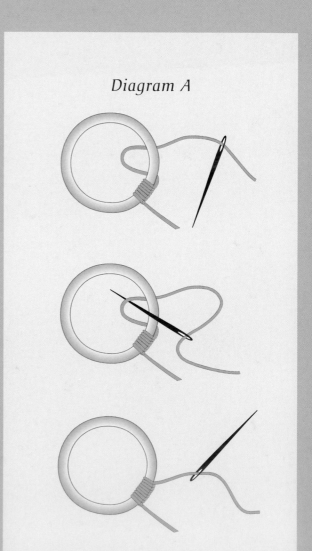

Diagram A

Shisha Rings with Sequins:

one Using two 27" strands of embroidery floss, tie floss around plastic ring with double knot, leaving 3" tail. Using chenille needle, thread long end of floss. Thread on sequins. Using crochet hook, crochet floss around ring, sliding one sequin down to ring every other stitch.

two Repeat Plain Shisha Ring Step 2 for finishing ring.

Suede

one Using pencil and ruler, draw one row of four 5" blocks onto suede for each repeat.

Blocks

Block 1:

one Fold one edge of velvet print under ½". Using straight pins, place and pin velvet square onto center of first marked suede block with folded edge on right and remaining sides over-hanging ½" past pencil lines.

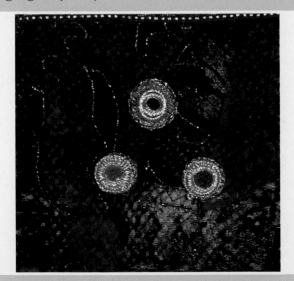

Block 2:

one Place piece of ⅜"-wide ribbon or trim horizontally at top of block, tucking ½" of raw edge under folded edge of velvet square. Place ⅜"-wide ribbon or trim below first ribbon or trim, tucking raw edge under velvet. Place 3"- and ¼"-wide ribbons or trims, leaving ½" space between 3"- and ¼"-wide ribbons or trims.

Block 3:

one Place and pin 1½"-, ¾"-, ⅞"-, and ⅜"-wide ribbon or trim vertically, leaving 1½" space between ¾"- and ⅞"-wide ribbons or trims.

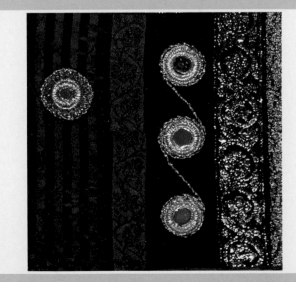

Embellished Panel Coat
Multiple Techniques
Diana Contine

Block 4:

one Place 1½"-wide pieces of ribbon or trim vertically on each side of block. Place second variety of 1½"-wide ribbon or trim horizontally at top of block. Place ⅝"-wide ribbon or trim horizontally at bottom of block.

two Using sewing machine, couch fabric, ribbons, and trims to suede. See Free-motion Stitching on page 18. Using darning foot and dropping feed dogs, free-motion stitch fabric, ribbons, and trims to secure.

Attaching Shisha Rings:

one Place shisha mirror on block. Place ring over mirror and using embroidery needle and metallic thread, buttonhole-stitch ring to fabric.

Optional: Embroider decorative stitches around some shisha rings as shown in Block 3 on page 25.

Fabric Care: Dry clean.

Chenille Blocks—
—Chenille and Machine Appliqué

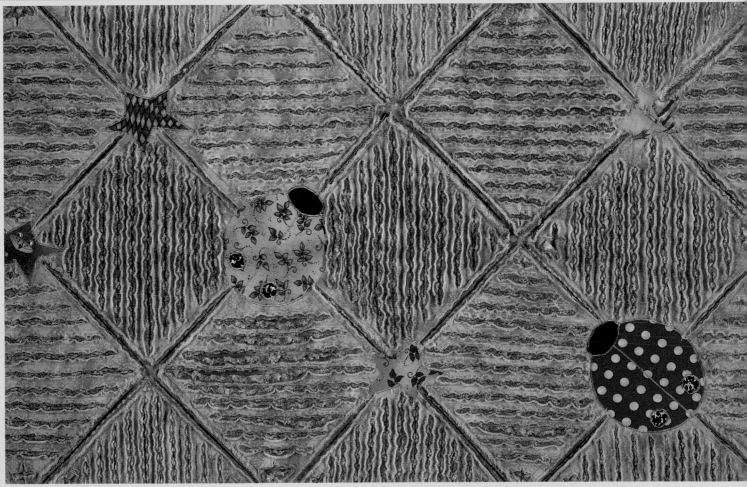

Fabric embellished by Mary Jo Hiney

Chenille is created by layering and stitching layers of fabrics onto a base cloth and cutting through the top layers between stitching. The fabric is then washed multiple times to create the chenille look.

Select varied fabric colors and patterns for layers. A green/purple print for the base cloth, orange/yellow and blue prints, and light blue variegated fabrics were used in the model. It is a good idea to place fabrics in desired order and sew a test square to see if the combination is effective.

Materials:

Fabrics:
    Cotton print scraps
    Cotton prints: four colors
Fusible webbing
Threads:
    Coordinating sewing
    Machine-embroidery

Basic Tools:

Iron and ironing board
Scissors:
    Embroidery
    Fabric
Sewing machine
Straight pins

Instructions

one Determine which fabric will be base fabric. Place base fabric right side up on smooth, flat work surface. Using fabric scissors, cut enough squares from each remaining fabric to cover base.

two Layer one of each colored fabric into separate square stacks. Place stacked squares on base cloth in a diamond pattern. Using straight pins, pin in place. *Note: Use half-diamonds as required on edges.*

three Using sewing machine, stitch each diamond and half-diamond ¼" from outside edge through all layers. Follow stitching directions as shown in Diagram A. Starting in center of diamond, stitch lines ½" apart. *Note: Back-stitching on stitches will save the number of threads that need trimming.*

four Using iron, fuse webbing onto wrong side of fabric scraps. Trace desired shapes onto paper side of webbing. Cut out shapes and remove paper backing. Fuse shapes onto several intersections between diamonds. Machine-satin-stitch shapes in place with embroidery thread.

five Using embroidery scissors, cut layered fabric in diamonds between stitches. *Note: Take care not to cut through backing. If this does occur, ladder-stitch backing together.*

six Machine wash and machine dry fabric. It may take two more washings and dryings to achieve desired look.

Note: Four layers are not a set number for the Chenille technique, additional layers will add more dimension and depth to a fabric.

Fabric Care: Machine wash in warm water and machine dry.

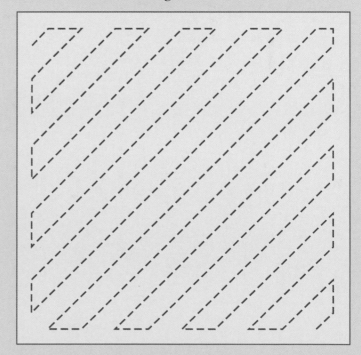

Diagram A

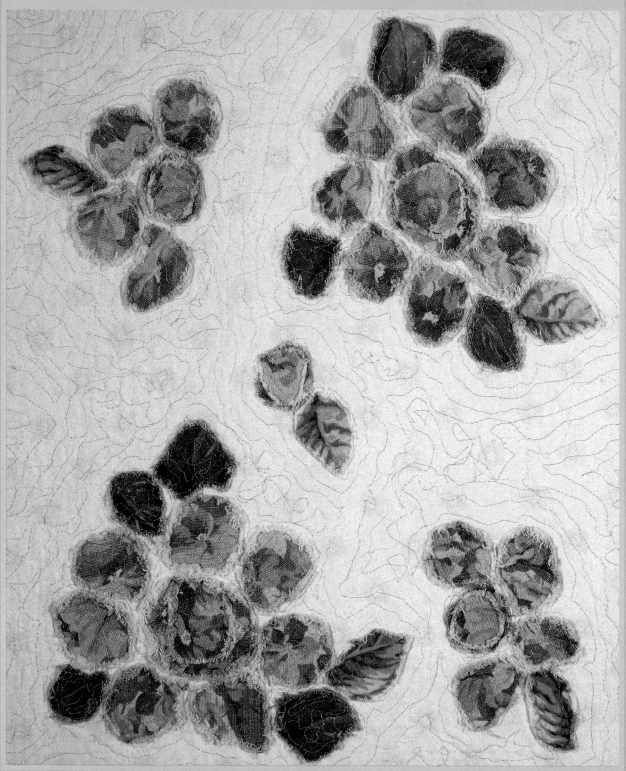

Frayed Flower Appliqué—
—Machine Appliqué and Free-motion Stitching

Materials:

Fabrics:
    Cotton drapery, floral print
    Cotton drapery, leaf print
    Cotton print: light-colored,
        subtle pattern
    Muslin
Sewing thread: metallic

Basic Tools:

Fabric scissors
Sewing machine with darning foot

Lace Appliqué
Mary Jo Hiney

Instructions

one Do not preshrink fabrics. Using scissors, cut out flowers from floral print. Cut out leaves from leaf print.

two See Free-motion Stitching on page 18. Place muslin right side down on smooth, flat work surface. Place cotton print right side up on muslin. Using straight pins, pin flower and leaf motifs onto cotton print and muslin, making certain to pin through all layers.

three Using sewing machine and darning foot, drop feed dogs and free-motion stitch ⅛" from edge around each flower and leaf with gold metallic thread. Randomly stitch inside shapes.

four Free-motion stitch around outside of flowers and leaves until background is covered with random stitching.

five Wash fabric in hot water and machine dry, allowing fabric flower designs to fray.

Fabric Care: Machine wash in warm water and machine dry.

Folded Jacket Patches—
—Appliqué and Fabric Origami

Fabric embellished by Mary Jo Hiney

Materials per Repeat:
Buttons: ¼"–⅜", assorted antique (5)
Embroidery flosses: assorted colors
Fabrics:
    Assorted scraps
    Cotton print
    Cotton print scraps: assorted (15)
Sewing thread: neutral

Basic Tools:
Embroidery needle: #3
Fabric scissors
Iron and ironing board
Sewing machine
Straight pins

Instructions

one   Tear cotton print fabric scraps for each jacket: 6" x 5½" piece for jacket, 6"x 5" piece for lining, 2½" x 3½" piece for inside shell.

two   Place jacket piece wrong side up on ironing board. Place lining piece on top of jacket with wrong sides together, aligning top and side edges. Place and center shell piece right side up ½" from jacket bottom. Fold jacket and lining to center as shown in Diagram A. Using iron, press in place. Fold bottom edge of jacket under ½" and press. Fold top inside corners of jacket and lining back for lapels and press as shown in Diagram B. Repeat for remaining jackets.

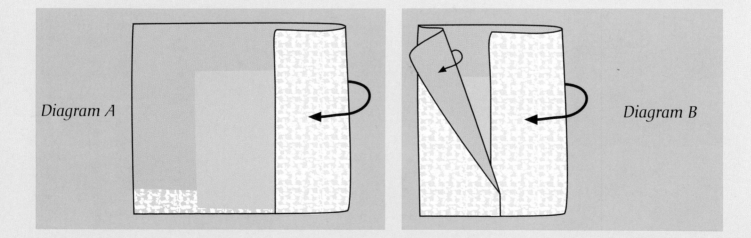

Diagram A

Diagram B

three Enlarge Leaf Patterns 200% and photocopy. Using straight pins, pin patterns onto assorted fabric scraps. Using scissors, cut out leaves.

four Pin jackets and leaves onto cotton print, allowing some leaves to overlap jackets. Leaves that are placed behind jackets need to be machine-stitched and/or hand-stitched, using three strands of floss and running stitch.

five Machine-stitch jackets to cotton print along inside of lapel fold line.

six Using embroidery needle and three strands of floss, buttonhole-stitch jackets onto fabric. Hand-stitch buttons at bottom of lapel.

Fabric Care: Hand wash in cold water and line dry.

*Leaf Patterns
Enlarge 200%*

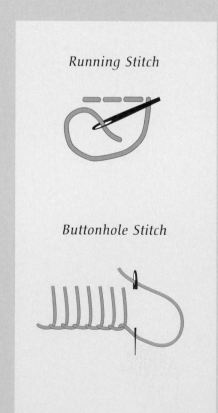

Running Stitch

Buttonhole Stitch

"Mmrow"
Appliqué and Origami Fabric
Mary Jo Hiney

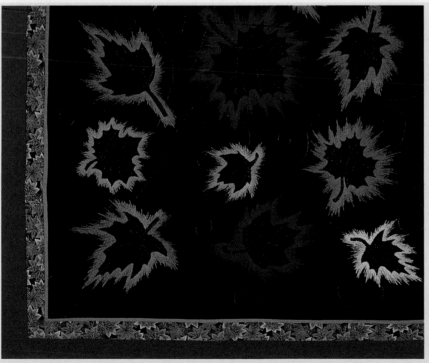

Machine Quilted and
Embroidered
Bobby Smead for Bernina

35

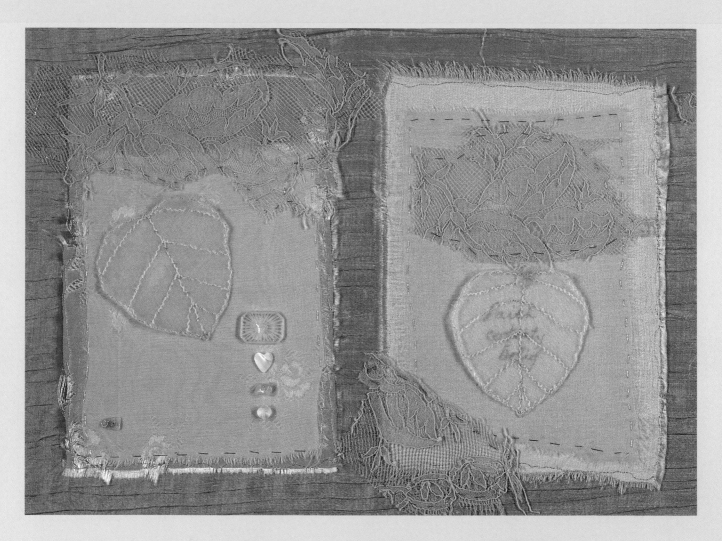

Leaves and Trinkets Collage—

—Appliqué and Machine Embroidery

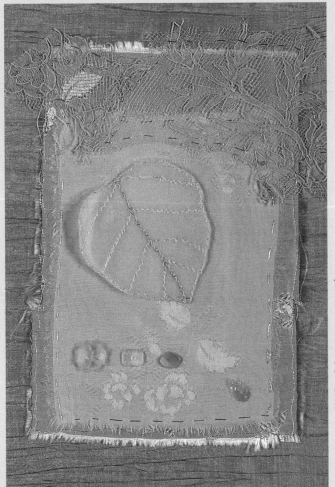

Faux collage is a technique that uses fabric and thread in place of paper to create a collage.

The transparent fabrics used for the collage over the krinkle taffeta in this model appear delicate and romantic. Pale gold brocade overlaid with off-white chiffon was used for the outside rectangle, while pale blue silk satin overlaid with pale gold chiffon was used for the inside. Pale blue, gold, and cream organdy was used to make the machine-embroidered leaves. Blush-colored Chantilly lace and trinkets that include clear glass, pale-toned stones, mother-of-pearl heart and leaves, and flower and rectangle buttons add the final accents.

Materials per Repeat:
Fabrics:
    Brocade
    Chantilly lace
    Chiffon: two colors
    Krinkle taffeta
    Organdy: three colors
    Silk satin
Sewing threads: metallic gold;
    off-white
Trinkets: ¼"–¾"

Basic Tools:
Fabric glue
Fabric scissors
Permanent ink gel pen: silver
    (optional)
Sewing machine with darning foot
Tissue paper

Instructions

one Tear two 5" x 7½" pieces from brocade. Tear one 5" x 7½" piece from satin. Fray all edges approximately ⅛".

Leaf Pattern

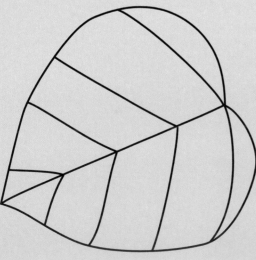

two Tear two 4½" x 6" pieces from one color chiffon and one from second color. Fray all edges ⅛".

three Tear small lace pieces to accent rectangles.

four Place satin piece vertically in center, and brocade pieces vertically on each side 1" apart on taffeta. See Free-motion Stitching on page 18. Using sewing machine, off-white thread, and darning foot, drop feed dogs and free-motion stitch rectangles to taffeta, stitching close to frayed edges.

five Place same color chiffon pieces over brocade rectangles. Using needle, doubled metallic gold thread, and running stitch, stitch chiffon in place. Place remaining chiffon piece over satin and stitch in place.

six Place torn lace as desired over chiffon pieces and stitch in place.

seven Trace Leaf Pattern onto tissue paper. Cut one piece of each color organdy ½" larger than leaf. Place organdy over leaf tracing on tissue paper. Using sewing machine, off-white thread, and darning foot, drop feed dogs and free-motion stitch organdy with narrow, wavy stitch onto tissue paper, following traced lines. Backstitch along stitching to avoid cutting thread until leaf has been completely stitched. Tear tissue away from leaf. Using scissors, trim leaf shape close to outside stitching.

eight *Optional: Using gel pen, write a few words or quote onto organdy where leaf will be attached.*

nine Using needle and metallic gold thread, stitch leaves to rectangles, following center vein.

ten Glue trinkets to rectangles.

Fabric Care: Hand wash in cold water and lay flat to dry. Do not wring.

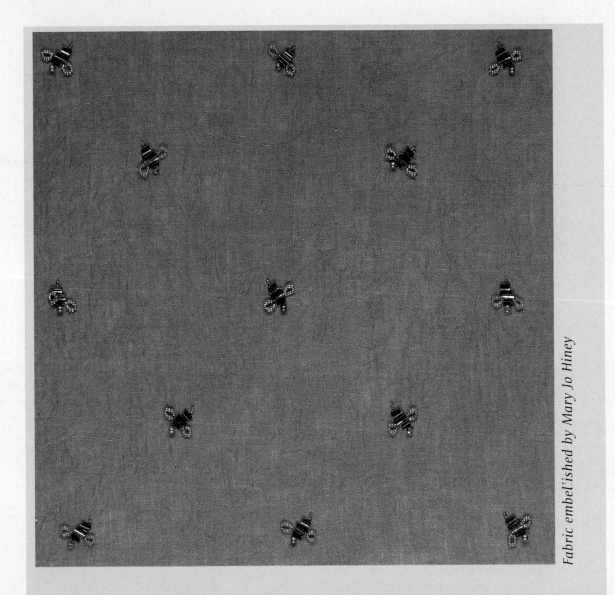

Fabric embellished by Mary Jo Hiney

Beaded Bumblebees—
—Bead Embroidery

Materials:

Linen fabric
Beads:
  Bugle: medium, black; metallic gold
  Bugle: small, black; metallic gold
  Faceted: 4 mm, amber
  Round: 4 mm, metallic gold
  Seed: petite, metallic gold
  Seed: standard, iridescent gold; metallic gold
Sewing threads: coffee; metallic gold

Basic Tools:

Embroidery hoop
Needles:
  Beading
  Sewing
Removable fabric marker: fine-tip
Ruler
Spray/mist water bottle

Instructions

one Using fabric marker and ruler, mark fabric into 5" squares. Mark bee head placement as shown in Diagram A.

two See Beading Basics on opposite page. Using beading needle and doubled coffee thread, bring needle up through fabric at bee mark and sew bee head and body as shown in Diagram B on opposite page. Stitch through each bead set a second time to secure. Vary round and faceted beads for bee heads.

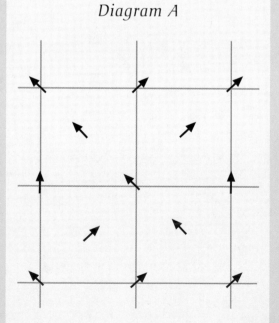

Diagram A

40

three Bring needle up through fabric at one end of medium gold bugle bead, thread ten standard metallic gold or ten iridescent gold seed beads onto needle and go down through fabric next to entry point as shown in Diagram C. Repeat for other wing. Vary use of metallic gold and iridescent gold beads for wings.

four Bring needle up through fabric behind last medium black bugle bead and thread on three petite seed beads for stinger.

five Using sewing needle, single gold metallic thread, and running stitch, stitch meandering trail on fabric surface.

six Using spray bottle, mist fabric and tightly crumple fabric with hands. Uncrumple fabric and allow to air dry.

Fabric Care: Hand wash in cold water and air dry.

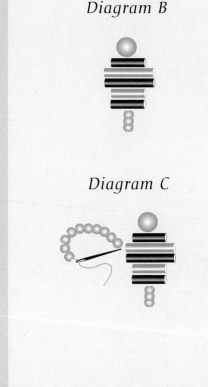

Diagram B

Diagram C

Beading Basics:

▨ When working with several colors and types of beads, place a small piece of velour or other plush fabric onto work surface. Pour a small amount of each bead onto cloth surface in separate piles. This will make the beads easier to work with and keep them from rolling around.

▨ Nylon beading thread or sewing thread is used for beading. Sewing thread can be strengthened by pulling through beeswax. Synthetic thread is a better choice than natural fibers because it does not deteriorate as quickly.

▨ Beading needle is threaded with doubled thread and knotted unless otherwise noted.

▨ Bring needle up through fabric at bead placement mark. Thread bead(s) onto needle and go down through fabric at end of bead set so that beads will lie flat against fabric. Stitch through each bead set a second time to give beads stability and shape.

▨ Wherever possible, carry thread on wrong side of fabric to the next bead position. Complete bead design before knotting thread on wrong side of fabric.

▨ Use a small embroidery hoop when beading motifs on lightweight fabric.

Beaded Dragonflies—
—Bead Embroidery

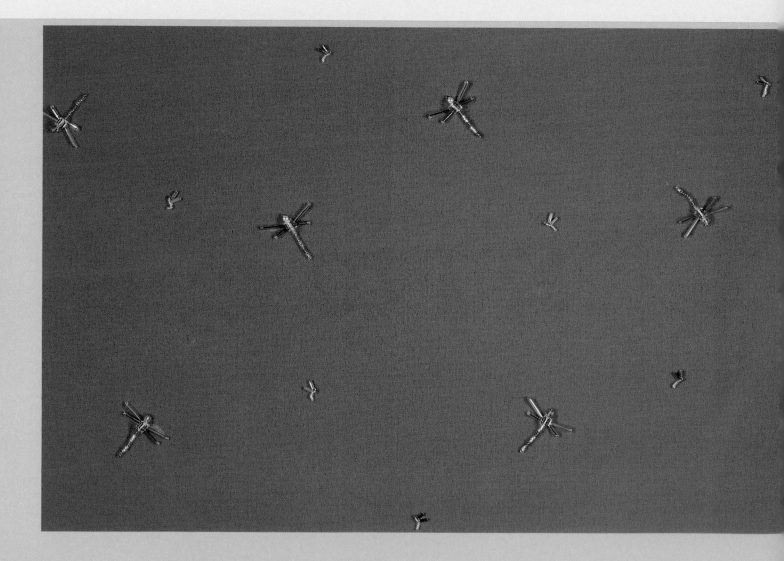

Necklace
Shell and Bead
Embroidery
Karen Perrine

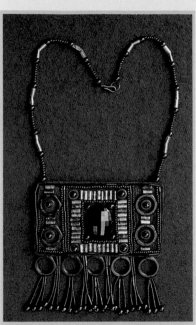

Necklace
Bead Embroidery
Karen Perrine

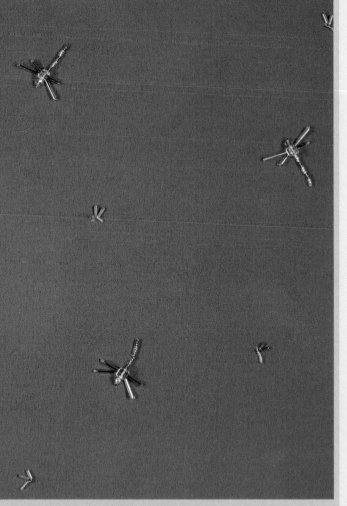

Fabric embellished by Mary Jo Hiney

The possibilities for beading on fabrics are limitless. Beading may take the form of delicate insects or become a geometric pattern. The types and styles of beads are abundant as well as the materials that they are made from.

The beaded dragonflies and tiny butterflies were formed from a variety of beads. A combination of 4 mm plain and faceted beads were used for the dragonfly heads. Translucent bugle beads in colors of mauve, sapphire, aqua, and blue gray, along with crystal pink standard seed beads were used to create the shimmery wings of the dragonfly. Crystal, faceted barrel beads were used for the body, while crystal blue and clear standard seed beads were used in combinations of three, and alternated for dragonfly bodies.

The tiny butterfly body is fashioned from aqua-colored petite crystal beads with a standard blue-colored crystal seed bead for the head. Wings are made with small peach and blue translucent bugle beads.

43

Materials:

Beads:
  Barrel faceted: 6 mm, crystal
  Bugle: large, translucent
  Bugle: medium, translucent
  Bugle: small, translucent
  Round: 4 mm, pearl
  Round faceted: crystal
  Seed: petite, crystal
  Seed: standard, crystal; crystal blue
Chiffon fabric
Sewing thread

Basic Tools:

Beading needle
Embroidery hoop
Removable fabric marker

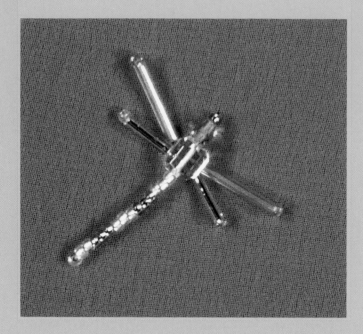

Diagram A

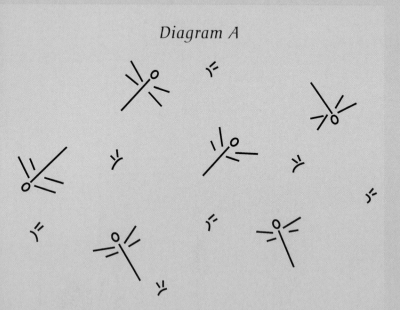

Instructions

one Using marker, mark placement on fabric for dragonfly and butterfly heads as shown in Diagram A.

two Using embroidery hoop, needle, and thread, bring needle up through fabric at dragonfly head mark. Thread on standard seed and 4 mm round pearl or faceted bead. Go down through fabric. Stitch through each bead set a second time to secure.

three Bring needle up through fabric by head and thread on barrel bead. Go down through fabric.

four Bring needle up through fabric near end of barrel bead and thread on three standard seed beads. Go down through fabric. Continue threading on three beads and attaching as shown in Diagram B on opposite page until fifteen beads have been attached. *Note: Use two colors of beads and alternate colors in groupings of three.*

Diagram B

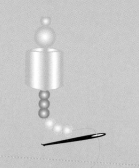

Diagram C

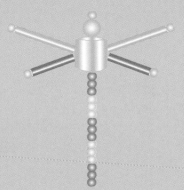

five Attach one large bugle and standard seed bead for upper wing as shown in Diagram C. Repeat for other side. Attach one medium bugle bead and standard seed bead below large bugle bead for smaller wing. Repeat for other side.

six Bring needle up through fabric at butterfly head mark. Thread on one small bugle bead for butterfly wing. Repeat for other wing

seven Bring needle up through fabric at butterfly head mark and thread one standard seed and seven petite seed beads onto needle. Go down through fabric, creating slight curve to beads as shown in Diagram D.

Fabric Care: Hand wash in cold water and line dry.

Diagram D

"Window in the Heart" Detail
Bead Embroidery and Appliqué
Karen Perrine

Beaded Flowers
Bead and Ribbon Embroidery
Mary Jo Hiney

Necklace
Bead Embroidery
Karen Perrine

Necklaces
Shell and Bead Embroidery
Karen Perrine

Beaded Lace—
—Bead Embroidery

esigns in laces vary dramatically, so these instructions will need to be adapted to suit each particular piece of lace. Outline-beading is used on outside sections of the model with an alternate outline-beading design used in center section. A beaded design was sewn over the rosette in the lace and can be easily adjusted to fit different sized flowers, rosettes, or other details.

Pearls from an old or broken necklace will add a rich and aged appearance to the lace. Using different shades of beads helps to eliminate the "glitzy" appearance of beading. The different bead shades will reflect a variety of light tones.

Materials:

Antique lace trim
Beads:
    Bugle: small, crystal
    Pearls: 2 mm, ecru
    Rondelle: 6 mm, crystal
    Round faceted: 4 mm, gold
    Seed: standard, champagne;
        lt. gold; silver; ivory
Sewing thread

Basic Tools:

Beading needle

Instructions

Outlined Lace Design:

one Determine beading outline.

two See Beading Basics on page 41. Using needle and doubled thread, bring needle up through lace at beginning of outline. Thread champagne, light gold, and champagne seed bead set onto needle. Go down through lace. Stitch through each bead set a second time to secure. Bring needle up through lace at end of bead set. Thread crystal bugle bead onto needle. Go down through lace. Continue pattern of seed bead set and bugles until lace has been outlined.

Alternate Outlined Lace Design:

one Follow Outlined Lace Design Steps 1–3, substituting silver for champagne and ivory for gold seed beads, and pearls for bugle beads.

Beaded Design:

one Determine lace areas for beaded designs.

two Using needle and doubled thread, bring needle up through lace near center of design. Thread three seed beads onto needle. Go down through lace at end of bead set. Stitch through each bead set a second time to secure. *Note: Design size will determine whether beads will need to be added or subtracted.*

three Bring needle up at center and repeat bead sequence, placing bead sets in wagon wheel formation. Continue design until area is covered.

four Stitch round faceted bead in center of design.

Alternate Beaded Design:

one Follow Beaded Design Step 3 for wagon wheel formation. Bring needle up through center and thread rondelle and gold seed bead onto needle and thread back through rondelle bead, allowing seed bead to sit on top of rondelle bead. Go down through lace in center of design.

Fabric Care: Dry clean.

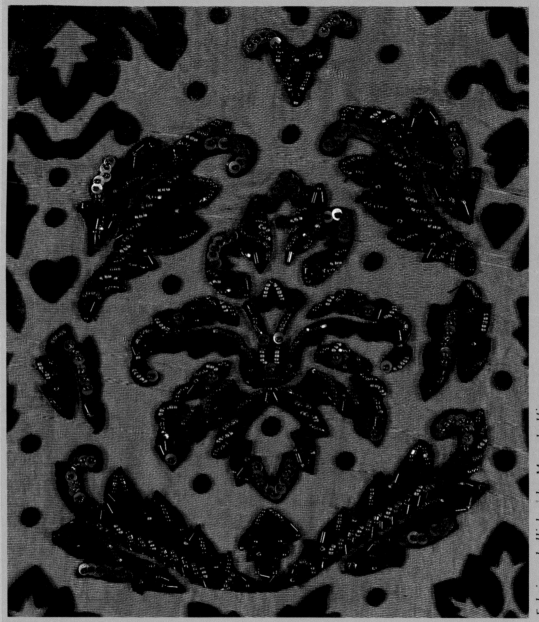

Fabric embellished by Mary Jo Hiney

Beaded Cut Velvet—
—Bead Embroidery

The most important aspect of beading fabric is to choose bead colors whose shades are beautiful together and enhance each other. Antique-gold-colored sequins with dark seed beads have a dramatic effect. Attaching one bugle bead will accomplish more with a single stitch than three seed beads, but using only bugle beads can be too predictable and mundane. Use the existing design, and determine bead combinations that will complement the design without covering it up.

Materials:

Beads:
    Bugle: small
    Faceted: 4 mm, two colors
    Seed: faceted
    Seed: standard, five colors
Cut velvet fabric
Sequins
Sewing thread

Basic Tools:

Beading needle
Embroidery hoop

Instructions

one Determine area on velvet to place beaded design. Determine where to place bead sets.

two Using needle and doubled thread, bring needle up through velvet and thread desired bead set onto needle. See Bead Basics on page 41. Go down through fabric. Stitch through each bead set a second time to secure.

three Repeat Step 2 for next bead set. Continue attaching bead sets as desired.

Ideas for Bead Combinations:

- Combine sequin and seed bead.
- Combine two bugle beads with faceted seed bead.
- Combine seed beads in color combinations.
- Combine seed beads in three, five, or six bead sets.
- Outline design with bugle beads, individually or near seed bead groups.
- Attach a seed bead to the fabric between two bugle beads.
- Attach faceted beads to the fabric in strategic locations to vary the effects of the beading and add accent.

Attaching Sequin and Bead Set:

Bring needle up through fabric. Thread sequin and seed bead onto needle. Thread needle back through sequin and fabric.

Tip: Use seed beads in simple color sequences, color patterns, or randomly.

Tip: Use a metallic bead as an accent at the beginning or end of a bead set.

Fabric Care: Dry clean.

Fabric embellished by Mary Jo Hiney

Beaded Diamonds—
—Bead Embroidery

Beaded and Hand-painted Scarves
Sandra Clark

Materials:

Beads:
    Rectangle: 4 mm x 10 mm, black
    Seed: standard, dk. iridescent
Cut velvet upholstery fabric: diamond–
    patterned
Metallic braids: fine, black; bronze
Sewing thread: black

Basic Tools

Beading needle
Sewing machine

Instructions

one Determine placement of black and bronze metallic braids along borders of diamonds. Using sewing machine and narrow zigzag stitch, with width of 1 and length of 3, couch braid onto fabric.

two See Beading Basics on page 41. Using beading needle and thread, bring needle up through fabric at center of four diamonds and thread on two seed beads, one rectangle bead, and two seed beads. Go down through fabric. Stitch through each bead set a second time to secure.

Note: Diamonds can be embossed onto velvet, using cotton cording and following Embossed Velvet Instructions on page 118.

Fabric Care: Dry clean.

Trail of Leaves—
—Bead and Hand Embroidery

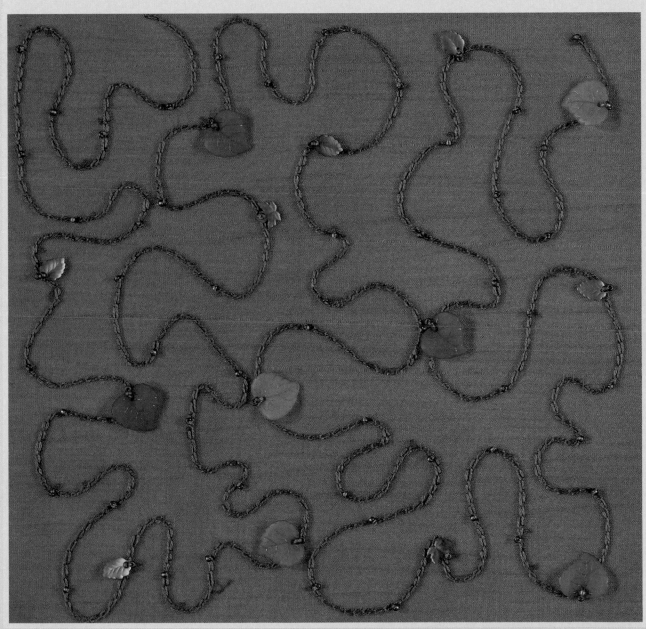

Fabric embellished by Mary Jo Hiney

Chiffon fabric
Embroidery floss
Glass specialty beads:
    Leaves: ¼"–⅜"
    Maple leaves: ⅜"
    Seed: standard, frosted
Leaf trinkets: ½"
Sewing thread

Embroidery hoop: small
Needles:
    Beading
    Embroidery: #5
Removable fabric marker: fine-tip

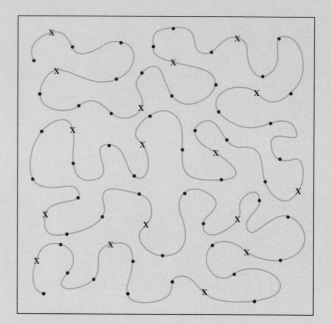

Diagram A

Chain Stitch

one Using fabric marker, draw desired chain-stitch pattern onto fabric as shown in Diagram A.

two Determine placement of specialty leaf beads and leaf trinkets by making "X" marks on fabric. Determine placement of individual seed beads by making three "•" marks between each "X" mark on fabric.

three Using embroidery hoop, embroidery needle, and two strands of floss, chain-stitch design. Using iron, press fabric when chain-stitching is completed.

four Using beading needle and thread, bring needle up through fabric surface at first "X" mark. Thread on leaf bead or trinket along with two frosted seed beads. Go down through leaf and fabric. Stitch through each bead set a second time to secure. Go down through fabric and weave thread through stitching on under-side of fabric to "•" mark. Bring needle up through fabric. Thread on standard seed bead. Go down through fabric. Continue attaching remaining beads and trinkets. When finished, trim thread close to chain-stitching as thread ends may show through chiffon.

Fabric Care: Hand wash in cold water and line dry.

"Salt Marsh Series No. 1"
Machine Embroidery
Martha Matthews

Martha Matthews graduated from Mary Baldwin College in Virginia, with a B.A. in Art History and Painting. She attended the Art Students League in New York City and has been weaving for twenty-seven years.

Her realistic and figurative tapestries have been in invitational and juried exhibitions in the United States, Canada, and Kenya. Her work has been featured in *Fiberarts*, *American Craft*, and *Shuttle, Spindle and Dyepot* magazines, as well as *The Fiberarts Design Books: One, Two, Four, and Six*. She has numerous works in private and corporate collections.

Martha has been active in the visual arts community in North Carolina and serves as their representative to the Southeast Region of the American Craft Council. She is an exhibiting member and former executive board member of the Piedmont Craftsmen.

The needle in her sewing machine has become her pencil with which she creates her realistic images on fabric. Her subject matter is derived from her world—the landscape of North Carolina or simple objects, such as bowl of pears.

Seashells and Beading—

—Bead and Machine Embroidery

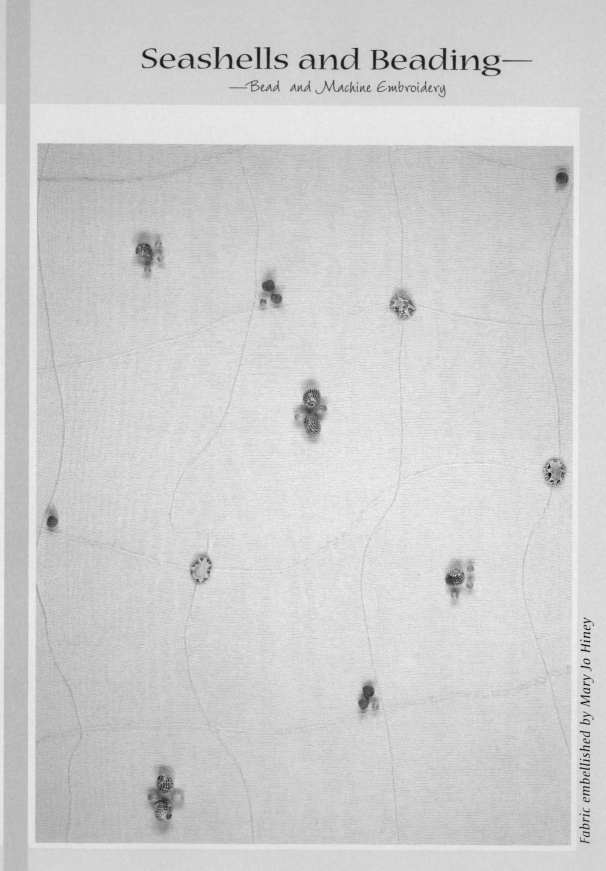

58

Materials:

Kite string: white
Scrim fabric
Seashells: small, assorted
Sewing thread: white
Wooden beads:
  6 mm, oval, natural
  6 mm, round, natural

Basic Tools:

Fabric glue
Fabric scissors
Sewing machine
Sewing needle

Instructions

one Using scissors, cut two equal lengths of scrim fabric and lay one on top of the other.

two Using sewing machine and narrow, zigzag stitch with width of 1 and length of 3, couch kite string onto the scrim in a 5"–6" uneven grid-like pattern.

three Using very thick fabric glue, randomly adhere seashells to fabric on grid centers, inner corners, and intersections. Refer to Beading Basics on page 41. Using needle and quadrupled thread, stitch wooden beads near groupings of seashells. Bring needle up through fabric at bead placement mark. Thread bead(s) onto needle. Go down through fabric at end of bead set so that beads will lie flat against fabric. Stitch through each bead set a second time to secure.

Fabric Care: Hand wash in cold water and line dry.

"Pear Series No. 10"
Machine Embroidery
Martha Matthews

Bead Bullions—

—Bead and Ribbon Embroidery

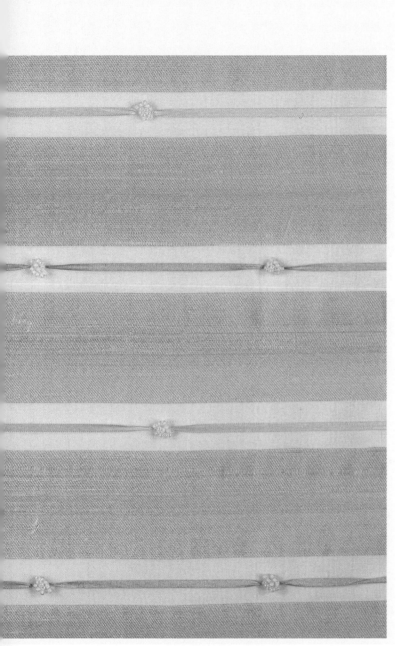

Fabric embellished by Mary Jo Hiney

Materials:
Seed beads: standard, four colors
Sewing thread
Sheer striped fabric
Silk Ribbon: 4 mm, two colors

Basic Tools:
Needles:
    Beading needle
    Embroidery needle: #3
Removable fabric marker: fine-tip

Materials:

one Using fabric marker, mark bead bullion placements 4" apart, along center of sheer portion on fabric, alternating every other row.

two See Beading Basics on page 41. Using beading needle and doubled thread, bring needle up through fabric and thread three seed beads of same color onto needle. Go down through fabric as shown in Diagram A. Stitch through each bead set a second time to secure.

three Bring needle up through fabric near beginning of first bead set and thread four seed beads of a second color onto needle as shown in Diagram B. Go down through fabric to the left of first bead set.

four Bring needle up through fabric near beginning of second bead set and thread five seed beads of a third color onto needle. Go down through fabric to the right of first bead set as shown in Diagram C. *Note: Vary use of seed bead colors suggested in Materials for each bullion.*

five Using embroidery needle and ribbon, bring needle up through fabric, beginning at outside edge of sheer stripe to lock ribbon. See Locking Ribbon and follow instructions for Step 2 on page 64. Go down through fabric underneath first bead bullion, keeping ribbon flat. Bring needle up through fabric on other side of bullion. Go down through fabric at next bullion. Continue stitching until other edge is reached and lock ribbon to secure.

six Using second color of ribbon, repeat Step 5, beginning under bullion at next stripe. Continue to alternate ribbon colors.

Fabric Care: Hand wash in cold water and line dry, or dry clean.

Diagram A

Diagram B

Diagram C

Pencil Violets—

—Bead and Ribbon Embroidery

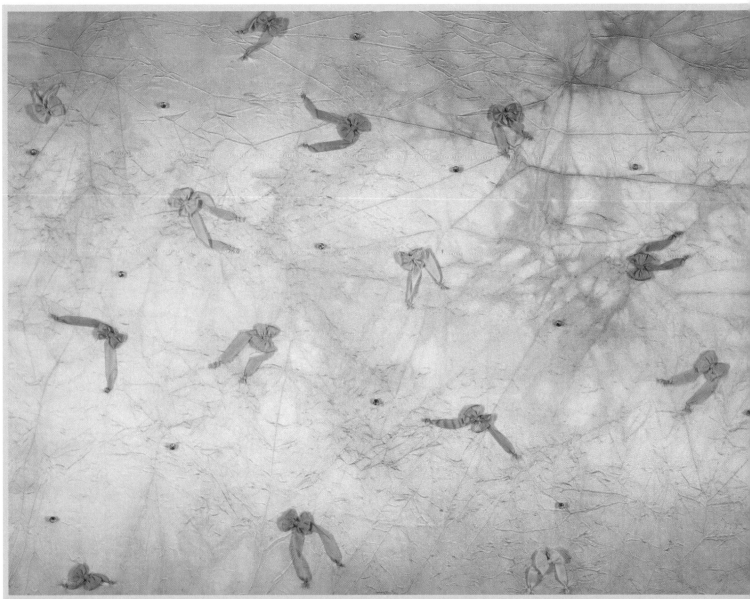

Fabric embellished by Mary Jo Hiney

Materials:

Beads:
    Round: 6 mm, clear with colored core
    Seed: standard, clear
Krinkle satin fabric: variegated
Sewing thread
Silk ribbons: 7 mm, 7 assorted colors (36" each)

Basic Tools:

Fabric scissors
Needles:
    Beading
    Chenille: #20
Sewing machine
Wooden pencils (2)

Instructions

Pencil Violets:

one Using scissors, cut ribbon into 18" lengths. Using two pencils held closely together, slip ribbon through center of pencils with one ribbon end extended 5". Weave ribbon around pencils so each pencil has three loops of ribbon as shown in Diagram A.

two Take top end of ribbon and wrap it down, under, and up between center of pencil. Pull ribbon tight, cinching center of ribbon loops together as shown in Diagram B.

three Take opposite ribbon end and wrap it up behind, over, and down as shown in Diagram C. Pull ribbon ends tight, cinching center of ribbon loops together and knot, creating violet as shown in Diagram D. Repeat Steps 1–3 for remaining ribbon lengths.

Embellishing Fabric:

one Using beading needle and thread, randomly tack knot of each violet 5" apart onto satin.

two Thread ribbon tail through chenille needle and lock ribbon. Allow ribbon to twist and go down through and out of fabric as show in Diagram E as shown on page 65. Stitch back down through and out of fabric parallel to first stitch as shown in Diagram F as shown on page 65. Trim ribbon ends to ⅛". Repeat for each ribbon end and violet. *Note: Vary lengths and direction of tails as shown in model.*

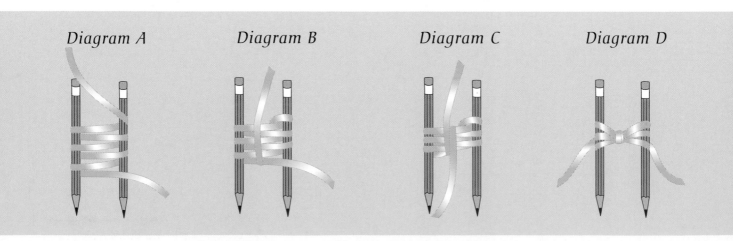

Diagram A   *Diagram B*   *Diagram C*   *Diagram D*

Victorian Lace Pillow
Ribbon Embroidery
Mary Jo Hiney

three Using beading needle and doubled thread, attach round beads in open spaces between violets. Bring needle up through fabric. Thread round bead and seed bead onto needle. Go down through fabric. Stitch through each bead set a second time to secure. Continue stitching beads onto fabric as desired.

Fabric Care: Hand wash in cold water and line dry.

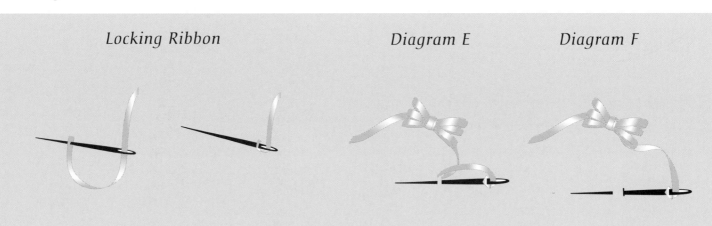

Locking Ribbon   *Diagram E*   *Diagram F*

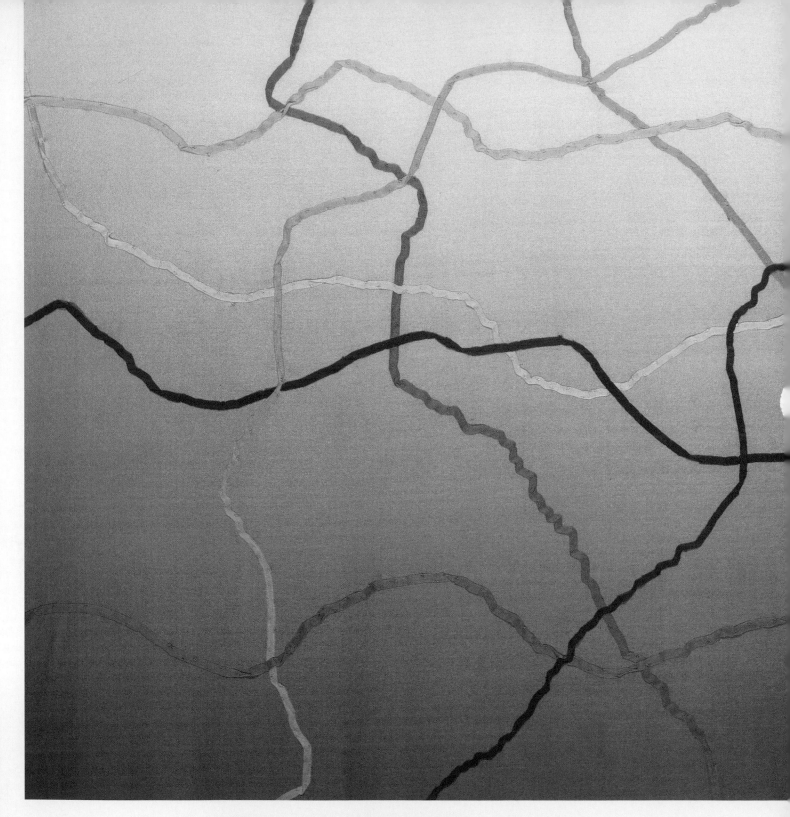

Road Map Ribbon—

—Ribbon Embroidery

Materials:

Sewing threads: coordinating with
    ribbons
Silk charmeuse fabric
Silk ribbons: 4 mm, assorted colors (8)

Basic Tools:

Iron and ironing board
Sewing needle

Instructions:

Using iron, press ribbons flat. Randomly pin ribbons onto fabric, curving and criss-crossing similar to road map pattern. Using needle and doubled thread, tack ribbon selvage onto fabric with very small stitches that alternate side to side. Remove pins as stitching is completed.

Press ribbon and fabric from back side. Ribbon will take on new curves and shapes.

Fabric Care: Hand wash in cold water and lay flat to dry, or dry clean.

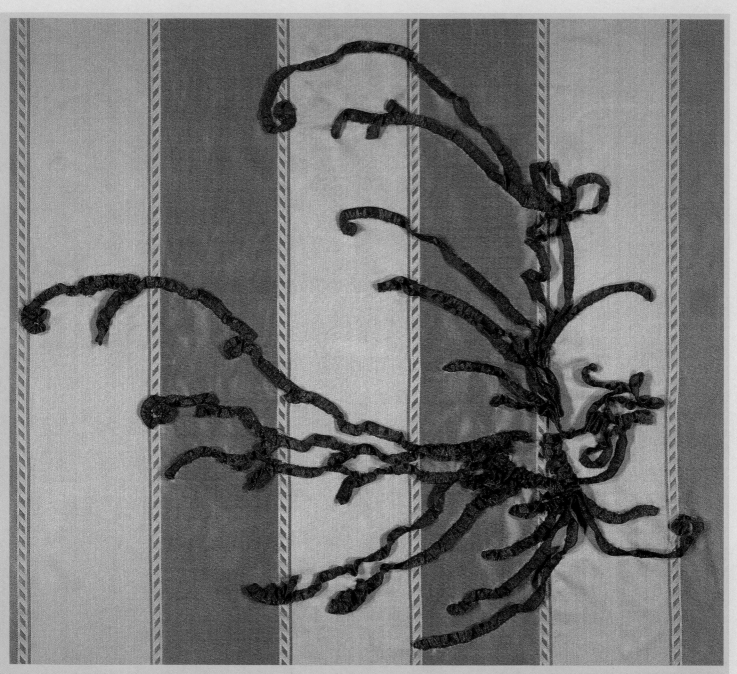

Fabric embellished by Mary Jo Hiney

Ribbon Rooster—
—Ribbon Embroidery

R ibbon is stitched on one gathered (ruched) edge, following a pattern that has been transferred to the fabric. The ribbon selected for edge-stitching should be a plain-weave ribbon that can be self-gathered. Ribbon can be tested for self-gathering by fraying ribbon end to expose the lengthwise fibers. Gently pull at a fiber near the selvage. If it begins to gather along the selvage and can be gathered down the length of the ribbon without breaking, it is self-gathering and will be suitable to use.

Materials:

Fabric
Ribbon: 9 mm, plain-weave (8 yds.)
Sewing thread

Basic Tools:

Fabric scissors
Light box or glass placed over light
    source
Needles:
    Darning: large-eye
    Sewing
Removable fabric marker
Straight pins

Victorian Lace and Ribbon Vest
Ribbon Embroidery
Mary Jo Hiney

69

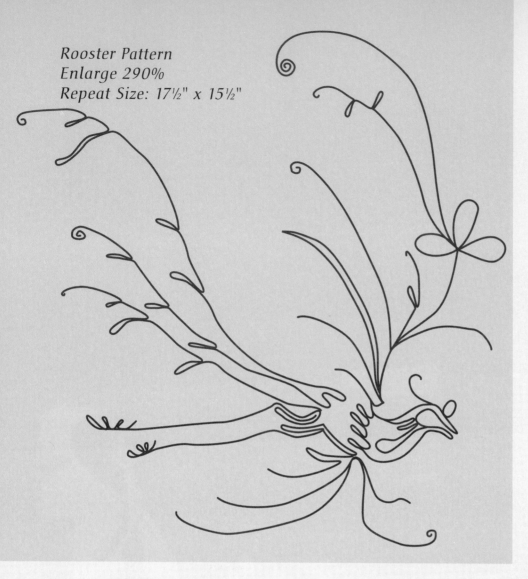

Rooster Pattern
Enlarge 290%
Repeat Size: 17½" x 15½"

gather. *Note: A slightly gathered 18" length would be approximately 13½".* Evenly space gathers along ribbon length.

four Using straight pins, pin gathered ribbon to fabric along design line. Using needle and doubled thread, hand-stitch ribbon along gathered selvage edge, alternating stitches from one side of ribbon to next so ribbon will be dimensional instead of lying flat.

five Continue stitching until 4" remain. Ungather remaining ribbon, thread ribbon into darning needle and go down through fabric. Using sewing needle and thread, tack ribbon in place on back, making certain stitches do not show on right side. Trim excess ribbon.

six Continue stitching gathered ribbon lengths to pattern lines until design is complete.

Alternative:

Using sewing needle and thread, ribbon could be hand-gathered or machine-gathered along the selvage edge of ribbon.

Fabric Care: Hand wash in cool water and air dry, or dry clean.

Instructions:

one Enlarge Rooster Pattern 290% and photocopy. Place fabric and pattern over light box. Using fabric marker, transfer pattern onto fabric.

two Using scissors, cut ribbon into 18" lengths. Using darning needle, thread ribbon and knot one end.

three Bring needle up through fabric at beginning of pattern line. Remove ribbon from needle. Fray ribbon end and gently pull fiber near the selvage, allowing ribbon to slightly

Ribbon Embroidery
Mary Jo Hiney

Pansies in Pockets—
—*Ribbon Embroidery*

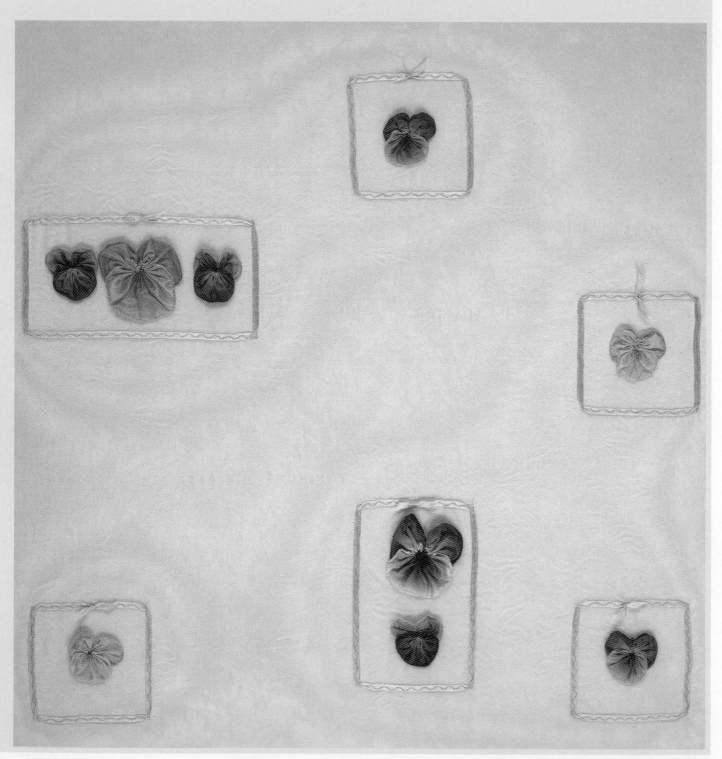

Fabric embellished by Mary Jo Hiney

Materials per Repeat:

Fabrics:
  Tulle: off-white (¼ yd.)
  Voile
Ribbons:
  Silk: 4 mm, lt. yellow (68")
  Wire-edged ombré ribbon:
    ⅝"-wide orchid (11")
    ⅝"-wide yellow (11")
    ⅝"-wide wine/lt. yellow (16½")
    ⅞"-wide orchid (8¼")
    ⅞"-wide dk. yellow/lt. yellow (8¼")
Sewing thread

Basic Tools:

Card stock
Pencil
Ruler
Scissors:
  Craft
  Fabric
Sewing machine
Sewing needle
Straight pins

Instructions:

one Using fabric scissors, cut two 5½" pieces of ⅝"-wide orchid ribbon, three 5½" pieces from ⅝"-wide wine/lt. yellow ribbon, and two 5½" pieces from ⅝"-wide yellow ribbon for small pansies.

two Using pencil and ruler, mark ribbon pieces at ¼", 1¾", 3¾" and 5¼" from one end, making five divisions. Fold ends at right angle as shown in Diagram A. Using needle and thread, gather-stitch around outside edge, starting at ¼" mark. Tightly gather ribbon and secure thread as shown in Diagram B. Join ends together to hide raw edges and shape petals as shown in Diagram C.

three Mark ⅞"-wide ribbon pieces at ¼", 2½", 5¾", and 8" from one end, making five divisions. Repeat Step 2 for making large pansies.

four Draw three patterns on card stock in the following dimensions: 2½" x 2½", 2½" x 4", and 2½" x 5". Using craft scissors, cut out templates. Trace four squares and one of each rectangle onto voile fabric.

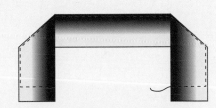

Diagram A

Diagram B

Diagram C

five Using pins, pin pansies to inside of traced squares and rectangles. Tack pansies in place.

six Using scissors and templates, cut out four squares and one each of rectangles 1" larger than templates from tulle. Place tulle pieces over pansies. Using sewing machine, stitch tulle along traced line on voile. Trim tulle close to stitching.

seven Using a narrow, wavy stitch, sew silk ribbon over traced lines and edge of tulle, beginning and ending at center top. Tie ribbon into knot and trim. Using iron, press from back side.

Fabric Care: Hand wash in cold water and line dry.

Fabric embellished by Mary Jo Hiney

Ribbon Bugs—
—Unique Ribbon Technique with Painted Background

Materials per Repeat:

Acrylic paints: leaf green; lt. green; pale green;
   yellow green; lt. rose; rose; white
Batting: lightweight, white (⅓ yd.)
Beads:
   Flat faceted: 4 mm (4)
   Round: 4 mm, assorted (2)
   Seed: standard (4)
Embroidery flosses: bright gold; lt. green;
   orange; orchid; red; white
Fabric paint medium
Fabric brush markers: mint green; rose
Felt: 2" x 2"
Linen: white

Ribbons:
   Grosgrain: ¼"-wide, variegated lilac (9")
   Grosgrain: ⅜"-wide, blue (9"); lime (9");
     orange (6"); turquoise (6")
   Satin: 1½"-wide, apricot (15"); blue (14");
     orange (5")
   Wired ombré: 1"-wide, green (10");
     green/blue (8"); orange (18");
     orchid (10"); dk. pink/orange (13");
     pink (13"); purple (5"); turquoise (5");
     dk. yellow (10")
   Wired ombré: 1½"-wide, green (11");
     lime green (5"); pink (18")
Sewing thread

Top

Flower and Vine Pattern
Enlarge 250%
Repeat Size: 23" x 11"

Basic Tools:

Fabric scissors
Flat paintbrush: ¼"-wide
Iron and ironing board
Light box or glass placed
    over light source
Needles:
    Beading`
    Embroidery: #5
    Sewing
Paint palette
Pencil
Sewing machine
Straight pins
Tape measure

Instructions

Painted Background:

one   Enlarge Flower and Vine Pattern 250% and photocopy. Place fabric and pattern over light box. Using sharp pencil, transfer pattern onto fabric.

two   Pour small amount of leaf green, lt. green, and pale green onto palette. Add enough paint medium so paint will spread easily. Test on fabric scrap. If necessary, add additional medium and test on fabric until proper consistency is reached.

three   Using paintbrush and green paint shades, lightly paint leaves, leaving some areas white. Dip paintbrush into clean water and with wet paintbrush, blend paint shades in leaves.

Repeat Step 2, using clean palette and lt. rose, rose, and yellow green.

Paint flowers with rose paint shades. Paint small amount of white on petals for shade variation. Paint flower centers with yellow green. Allow paint to dry.

Using rose fabric marker, outline left side of each flower petal. Using green fabric marker, outline leaf shape, center, and stems. Draw details on flower centers.

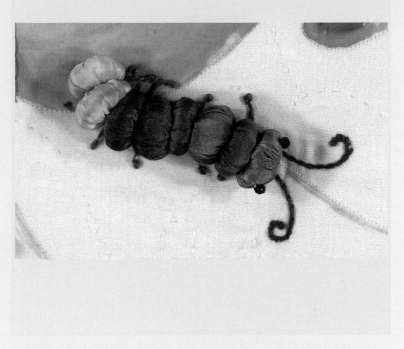

Using iron and following manufacturer's instructions for fabric paints, press fabric to set design.

Place painted fabric on light-weight batting and using straight pins, pin together. Machine-stitch with white thread around painted design.

Using embroidery needle, three strands of white floss, and running stitch, stitch meandering trail around flowers and leaves throughout fabric background. Do not stitch through painted flowers and leaves.

Ribbon Bugs
Caterpillar:

Cut two 5" pieces each from orchid, pink, and pink/orange 1"-wide ombré ribbon and one piece each from purple and turquoise 1"-wide ombré ribbon for body sections (turbans). Slide back selvage to expose and remove wires. Discard wires. *Note: The best ombré ribbon shades are wired. Another type of unwired ribbon, such as polyester, may be substituted.*

Fold ribbon in half widthwise and match cut edges. Machine-stitch edges together and turn right side out, making tube. Using sewing needle and thread, gather-stitch selvage on one end of tube. Pull gathers to close off end and secure. Gather-stitch selvage on open end and stuff with small amount of batting. Pull to close. Secure thread, pull through opposite side, and cut. Repeat with remaining ribbons.

Arrange body sections, starting with turquoise, then purple, pink/orange, orchid, and pink. Attach body sections by passing needle and thread through centers and securing.

Using beading needle and doubled thread, attach two faceted beads onto front section of caterpillar for eyes.

Using sewing needle and thread, tack caterpillar onto quilted background. Using embroidery needle and six strands of orange floss, pistil-stitch legs. Outline-stitch antennas with three strands of red floss.

Honey Bee:

one Cut two 5" pieces from dk. yellow and three 5" pieces from orange 1"-wide ombré ribbon for body sections (turbans). Repeat Caterpillar Step 2 for making body sections. Repeat Caterpillar Step 3 for arranging and attaching body sections, beginning with orange and alternating between orange and yellow.

two Using beading needle and doubled thread, attach eyes.

three Cut one 5" piece each from green and lime green 1½"-wide ombré ribbon. Using sewing needle and thread, gather-stitch around ribbon as shown in Diagram A and secure.

four Place bee body on background. Place wings behind bee body to hide raw edges and shape. Using embroidery needle and two strands of lt. green floss, tack wings in place. Randomly tack inside of wings with bright gold floss.

five Using sewing needle and thread, tack bee body onto quilted background. Using embroidery needle, six strands of orange floss, and chain-stitch with long tack-stitch, stitch legs and stinger. Outline-stitch antennas with six strands of orange floss.

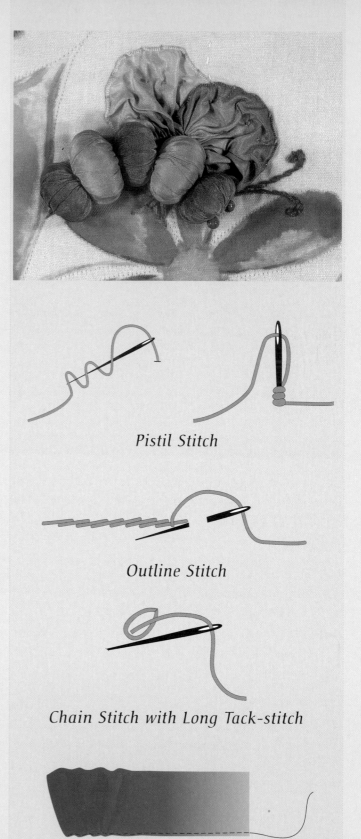

Pistil Stitch

Outline Stitch

Chain Stitch with Long Tack-stitch

Diagram A

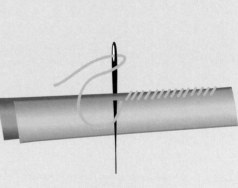

Diagram B

Dragonfly:

one   Cut three 3" pieces from blue and two 3" pieces from turquoise ⅜"-wide grosgrain ribbon, one 3" piece from lilac ¼"-wide grosgrain ribbon, and one 3" piece from green/blue 1"-wide ombré ribbon for body. Remove any wires from selvages.

two   Using sewing needle and thread, place right sides of blue and turquoise ribbon pieces together, matching up selvage edges. Using embroidery needle and two strands of lt. green embroidery floss, whipstitch one side of selvage edges together as shown in Diagram B. Open up ribbon and finger-press flat.

three   Place right side of second piece of blue ribbon to unstitched edge of turquoise and whipstitch together. Whipstitch blue to second turquoise. Place lilac ¼"-wide grosgrain on top of green/blue 1"-wide ombré ribbon, matching edge on one side. Place matched ribbon edges on edge of blue ribbon and whipstitch together.

four   Smooth out stitched ribbons and fold in half lengthwise with right sides together. Machine-stitch along selvage edge, tapering to point, and trim ⅜" seam on ribbon. Turn right side out and stuff with batting. Gather-stitch open end, pull to close, and secure thread. Tightly wrap two strands of embroidery floss twice around body 1" from top.

five   Cut one 5" piece from green/blue 1"-wide ombré ribbon for head. Repeat Caterpillar Step 2 for making body sections. Repeat Caterpillar Step 3 for attaching head to body section.

six   Using beading needle and doubled thread, thread flat bead and seed bead onto needle for eye. Take needle back through flat bead and secure. Repeat for remaining eye.

seven Cut two 5" pieces from 1"-wide apricot satin ribbon and two 7" pieces from blue satin ribbon for wings. Fold ribbons as shown in Diagram B. Using needle and thread, gather-stitch across bottom of folded ribbon. Pull thread tight as shown in Diagram C. Wrap around bottom of ribbon, and secure. Repeat for remaining wings.

eight Place dragonfly body on background. Place blue wings on background near top of body behind bee body to hide raw edges and shape. Tack in place. Place apricot wings, overlapping blue wings, on background and tack in place.

nine Using embroidery needle and six strands of bright gold embroidery floss, outline-stitch antennas.

Snail:

one Cut two 3" pieces from lilac ¼"-wide grosgrain ribbon, two pieces from orange ⅜"-wide grosgrain ribbon, and one 3" piece each from orange, pink, and dk. pink/orange 1"-wide ombré ribbons. Remove any wire from selvages.

two Using embroidery needle and two strands lt.

Diagram B

Diagram C

green floss, repeat Dragonfly Steps 1–2, for whipstitching dk. pink/orange with lilac ribbon to orange grosgrain ribbon. Whipstitch orange ombré and lilac ribbons to orange grosgrain ribbon. Whipstitch orange grosgrain ribbon to orange ombré ribbon. Whipstitch orange ribbon grosgrain to pink ombré ribbon.

Cut one 5" piece from green 1"-wide ombré ribbon. Repeat Dragonfly Steps 5–6 for making head. Using sewing needle and thread, tack snail onto quilted background.

Cut one 18" piece from 1½"-wide pink ombré ribbon. Coil ribbon and place on felt. Tack coil near outer edges and center of ribbon to felt. Trim excess felt around ribbon. Place coiled ribbon on background. Overlap coiled ribbon onto snail body and background. Fold back raw edges and using embroidery needle and bright gold floss, tack coil at outer edges and in center to secure. Outline-stitch antennas with six strands of orchid floss.

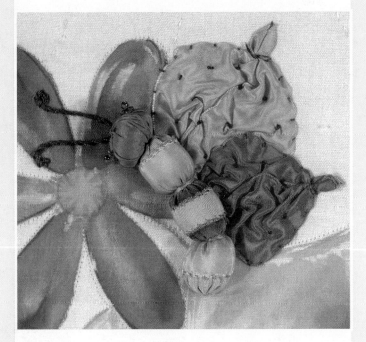

Butterfly:

Cut three 3" pieces from lime green ⅜"-wide grosgrain ribbon and two from green 1½"-wide ombré ribbon. Remove any wire from selvages.

Using embroidery needle and two strands lt. green floss, repeat Dragonfly Steps 1–2 for whipstitching lime green grosgrain ribbon to green ombré ribbon. Continue whipstitching body together, alternating grosgrain and ombré ribbons. Tie off body into three equal sections with embroidery floss.

Cut one 5" piece from green 1"-wide ombré ribbon. Repeat Dragonfly Step 5 for making head. Repeat Dragonfly Step 6 for attaching faceted and seed beads to head.

Cut 5" piece each of orange and apricot 1½"-wide satin ribbon. Repeat Dragonfly Step 8 for making wings. Place butterfly body onto background. Place orange wing onto background near top of body behind bee body to hide raw edges. Pinch wing tip and tack wing in place. Repeat with remaining wing.

Using sewing needle and doubled thread, tack body onto quilted background, covering raw edges of wings.

Fabric Care: Dry clean.

Sponge Over Pattern—
—Fabric Sponge Painting

S ponge-painting over commercially printed patterns can create a new fabric design as well as make the existing pattern more subtle. Household sponges purchased at the supermarket work the best because of the randomly sized and shaped holes.

Materials:

Cotton print fabric
Fabric paint

Basic Tools:

Disposable spoon
Flat tray or lid
Household sponge
Iron and ironing board
Masking tape
Paper towels
Small bowl

Instructions

one Using iron, press fabric to remove wrinkles and creases. Using masking tape, tape fabric edges right side up on smooth, flat work surface.

two Wet sponge and squeeze out water. Roll sponge in paper towel and squeeze flat to remove any excess water.

three Pour paint into bowl and slightly thin with water. Using spoon, place thin layer of paint on one side of tray. Dip damp sponge into paint and tap flat on tray, rotating sponge all directions to evenly distribute paint. Holes in sponge should be open. Press sponge on fabric. Sponge color on in layers until desired coverage is reached. Allow paint to dry to the touch. *Notes: Light pressure produces speckles and more pressure produces heavier coverage. Sponge can be pressed on fabric a number of times before adding more paint to sponge.*

four Remove fabric from surface. Drape or hang fabric and allow to air-dry for 24 hours. Press on wrong side of fabric to set paint.

Fabric Care: Machine wash and machine dry.

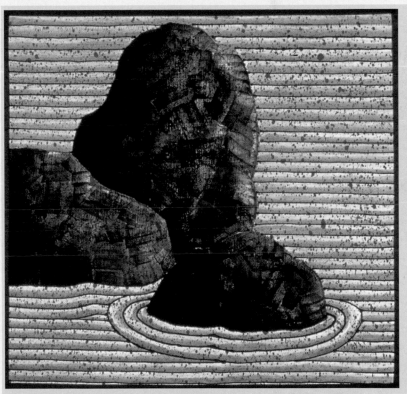

"Rock Garden"
Dye, Paint, Hand- and Machine-quilted
Karen Perrine

Background Painting—
—Fabric Painting and Blending

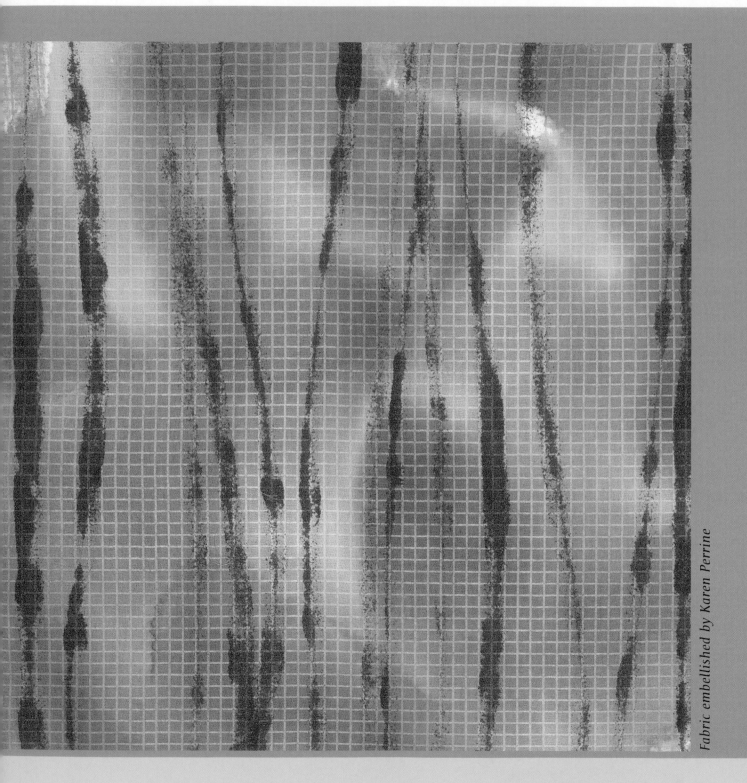

Fabric embellished by Karen Perrine

Many of the basic tools for this technique can be found around the house. House trim paintbrushes may be substituted for acrylic paintbrushes and empty yogurt or margarine containers will be perfectly suitable for mixing paints.

Materials:
Fabric: white pattern on white
Fabric paints: three colors; one metallic

Basic Tools:
Acrylic paintbrushes: flat, ¼"–1" or
    house trim paintbrushes 1½"–2½"
Disposable plastic bowl
Disposable plastic spoons
Masking tape

Instructions

one Using masking tape, tape test fabric edges right side up on smooth, flat surface.

two Squeeze paint into bowl and add small amount of water. Using spoon, mix paint and water until blended. Using paintbrush, test paint on piece of fabric for color-blending.

Successful color-blending on fabric is dependent on the amount of water mixed with the paint or pigment. The secret is to mix the paint thin enough to flow, but thick enough so that it is controllable. Color blending occurs when brush strokes meet or cross. It is always best to test paint on scrap fabric before beginning.

three Using iron, press fabric to remove wrinkles and creases. Tape fabric edges right side up on smooth, flat surface.

four Paint fabric as desired. Allow to dry to the touch.

five Paint surface with metallic paint, using random strokes. Allow to dry to the touch.

six Remove fabric from surface. Drape or hang fabric and allow to air-dry for 24 hours. Press on wrong side of fabric to set paint.

Fabric Care: Machine wash and machine dry.

Painting Variations:
- Make long brush strokes while twisting paintbrush.
- Place pools of different colored paints on damp fabric and allow the colors to blend.
- Paint different colored strokes, touching side-by-side for color blending.

"Night Rocks"
Dye and Paint, Dye Discharge, Piecing,
Hand- and Machine-quilted
Karen Perrine

Sponge Pattern—
—Fabric Sponge Printing

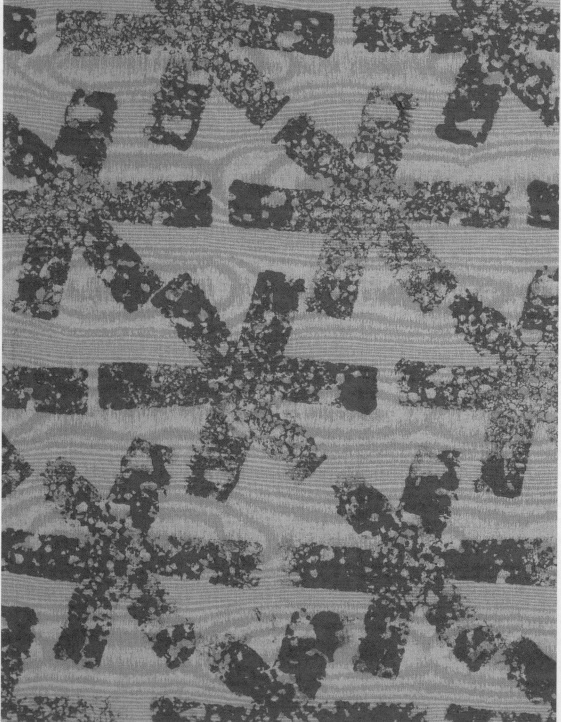

Fabric embellished by Karen Perrine

Karen Perrine grew up in eastern Washington state, in a farming and quilting family. She began sewing as soon as she could reach the foot control on the sewing machine. She graduated from Washington State University with a major in Chemistry and a minor in Art.

Karen is a surface designer and paints, prints, embroiders, and manipulates fabric to create unique jewelry, wall hangings, and garments. She has exhibited her art throughout the United States. She received the *Award of Excellence* at Quilt National '95 and has had the quilt "POOL" on tour with Quilt National '97.

Karen has taught design and fiber techniques in her home state of Washington as well as Louisianna, Maine, Montana, New York, and Oregon.

Shapes can be sponge-printed over patterned or solid-colored fabric. Shapes can printed randomly or in a repetitive pattern. Use one or several coordinating fabric paint colors.

Materials:
Fabric
Fabric paint

Basic Tools:
Bowl
Disposable spoon
Flat tray or lid
Household sponge
Iron and ironing board
Masking tape
Paper towels
Scissors

Instructions

one Using iron, press fabric to remove wrinkles and creases. Place fabric right side up on smooth, flat surface. Using masking tape, tape fabric edges in place.

two Wet sponge and squeeze out water. Roll sponge in paper towel and squeeze flat to remove excess water.

three Using scissors, cut sponge into desired shape.

four Pour paint into bowl and slightly thin with water. Using spoon, spoon thin layer of paint to one side of tray. Dip damp sponge into paint and tap flat on tray in all directions to evenly distribute paint. Holes in sponge should be open. Press sponge on fabric. Allow paint to dry to the touch. *Notes: Light pressure produces speckles and more pressure produces heavier coverage. Sponge can be pressed on fabric a number of times before adding more paint to sponge. Tip: Larger shapes print more evenly by using flat, wooden block to press down on sponge.*

five Remove fabric from surface. Drape or hang fabric and allow to air-dry for 24 hours. Press on wrong side of fabric to set paint.

Fabric Care: Machine wash and machine dry.

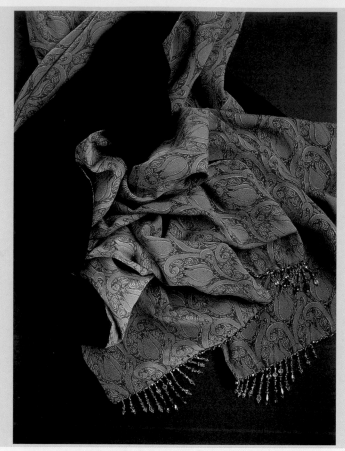

Velvet Scarf
Stenciled Velvet with Beaded Fringe
Diana Contine

Panel Coat/Vest
Embellished fabric
Diana Contine

Diana Contine creates one-of-a-kind designs in hats, clothing, and wire-wrap sterling silver jewelry under her own label, Dakota Moon.

She began as a graphic designer, then went into nursing for financial reasons. Following a work-related back injury, she decided to begin a new career. Diana worked part-time reproducing vintage clothing. She began making soft toys, which led into rompers for children, then developed into adult clothing.

Diana has an Associate degree in Design and Commercial Art from Florissant Valley Community College, followed by an Associate degree in Nursing from St. Mary's College of Nursing. She received her B.S. in Interior/ Environmental Design from Eastern Michigan University. She has taken courses in Millinery Design from Moore College of Design, and Design and Architectural Historical Renovation from American College in London, as well as workshops in metal techniques from Horizons New England School of Crafts. Diana was accepted into both the Pennsylvania and Buck County Guilds of Craftsmen.

Weekends find her packing her RV with racks of clothing, jewelry displays, and hat stands for fairs and festivals.

Jane Dunnewold chairs the Design Department at the Southwest School of Art and Craft in San Antonio, Texas. She is the author of two books, *Complex Cloth* and *Fifteen Beads*. Her work is centered on the notion of art cloth—fabric which has been layered with dyes, paints, and other media as a way of achieving a visually rich and complete surface.

Jane maintains a studio in San Antonio. She has been included in numerous national exhibitions, including Quilt Nationals '93, '95, and '97 as well as in Visions San Diego '95 and '97.

Jane seeks for depth and complexity in cloth surfaces and creates this effect by layering color and pattern with dyes, paints, stamps, silkscreens, and miscellaneous other tools. She thinks of these pieces as "spirit cloth", because each piece is imbued with its own personality which draws not only from her soulwork, but from elements that sustain her—the gifts and relics of the natural world. Jane's challenge for her art is to honor that which inspires—to represent it in a way that is visually poetic.

Yardage
Embellished Fabric
Jane Dunnewold

Yardage
Embellished Fabric
Jane Dunnewold

Stencil Painting—
—Fabric Stenciling

Fabric embellished by Karen Perrine

Small, house trim foam paint rollers are used over thin hand-cut templates to produce individual or repetitive patterns. Precut stencils are too thick for the roller to fill in the corners or detail areas and also create fuzzier edges.

Foam rollers that are denser and less sponge-like, such as rollers with white foam material, work best for stenciling with a roller.

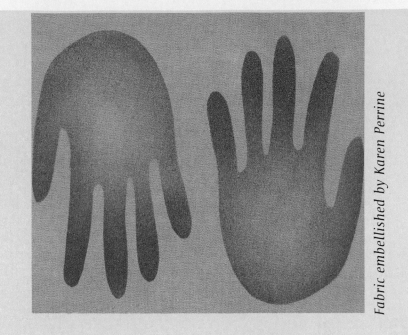

Fabric embellished by Karen Perrine

Materials:
Fabric or ribbon
Fabric paint

Basic Tools:
Artist's acetate sheet
Craft knife
Cutting mat
Disposable spoon
Flat tray or lid
Iron and ironing board
Masking tape
Paper towels
Permanent marker: ultrafine-tip
Scratch paper
Small house trim foam paint roller

Instructions

one Using marker, draw design onto scratch paper. Place acetate on paper and trace design onto acetate. *Note: Leave 2" margin of uncut acetate around cut design area.* Using masking tape and craft knife, tape acetate to cutting mat and carefully cut out design areas. *Note: If a mistake is made when cutting out stencil, repair with masking tape on underside of acetate.*

two Using iron, press fabric or ribbons to remove wrinkles and creases. Tape fabric edges right side up on smooth, flat surface. Tape stencil on fabric.

three Place wide layer of paint across one end of tray. Using paint roller, dip into paint bit by bit to evenly distribute thin layer of paint. Make several passes across tray to finish distributing paint. *Note: If holes in foam do not show, there is too much paint on roller.* Roll paint across paper towel to check if paint is distributed evenly.

four Lightly roll paint onto fabric. First pass will be light dots of color. Continue to lightly roll over stencil until desired coverage is achieved. *Note: Avoid placing too much paint on fabric. If paint surface looks shiny, too much has been applied.* Lift tape and stencil from fabric surface and reposition for next repeat. *Note: If necessary, lay paper towel over damp paint before repositioning stencil.*

five Allow paint to dry to the touch before removing fabric from work surface. Allow fabric to air-dry for 24 hours. Press on wrong side of fabric to set paint.

Fabric Care: Machine wash and machine dry.

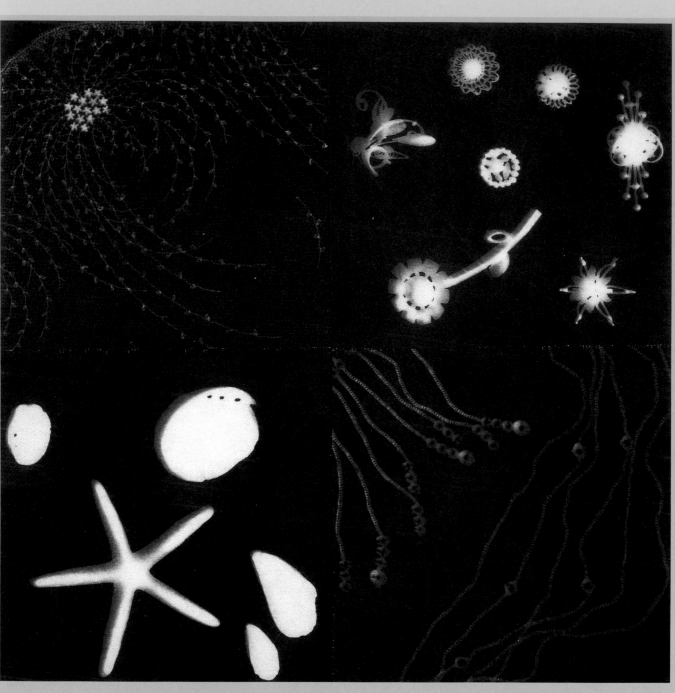

Fabric embellished by Mary Jo Hiney

Natural Blueprints—
—Blueprinting

The fabric used for this technique has been treated with a blueprint photographic chemical and is available in several types of fabrics and colors. The white fabric produces white prints with a Prussian blue background, fuchsia fabric produces fuchsia prints with a purple background, and turquoise fabric produces turquoise prints with a dark blue background.

Small squares and pieces of fabric, such as the 10" squares used in the model, are the most convenient to set up. Multiple pieces may be done by setting up one piece while another is blueprinting.

Seashells, jewelry, lace, and beaded fringe were used as blueprinting objects in the model. Seashells and jewelry created the largest white spaces, while fine lace and beaded fringe created delicate, light blue images. When selecting blueprinting objects, keep in mind that large, flat objects will create larger white spaces without shadow. Objects that have some curve will allow sunlight to creep under edges producing a shadow effect. Test objects in sunlight on scrap pieces of fabric to check their effect for shadows.

Materials:
Blueprint-treated cotton fabric

Basic Tools:
Blueprinting objects
Cardboard box: same size or larger
    than foam-core board or
    Styrofoam®
Craft knife
Foam-core board or Styrofoam®:
    ¼" larger than fabric
Straight pins
Timer

Instructions

one Turn cardboard box so that open side is facing down. Using straight pins, pin foam-core board to cardboard box. Remove piece of blueprint fabric from storage bag in low light and pin securely on foam-core board. *Tip: It is important that fabric is secured to box. Fabric that lifts up or wrinkles will not blueprint evenly.*

two Arrange blueprint objects on fabric as desired. Place fabric and box outside in direct sunlight. Set timer at 10 minutes for warm, sunny day; 15 minutes for cool, sunny day; and 20 minutes for cold, bright day. *Note: Manufacturer's instructions may have more detailed information.*

three Bring fabric and box inside to low light and remove blueprint objects. Immediately rinse fabric with cold water until water runs clear to fix design. Allow to dry.

Fabric Care: Hand wash in liquid dish soap or laundry detergent that does not contain phosphates or soda products and machine dry.

Stenciled Velvet—
—Theorem Painting

Fabric embellished by Mary Jo Hiney

heorem painting was originally stencil painting done on velvet, using oil paints. Theorem painting has progressed to stencil painting on various fabrics and using various permanent paint mediums.

Materials:

Cotton velvet fabric
Fabric paints: leaf green; lt. leaf green

Basic Tools:

Iron and ironing board
Masking paper
Masking tape
Paint palette
Stencil: leaf spray design, purchased or
    hand-cut
Stencil brushes: ¼" (2)

Instructions

one Using iron, press velvet on wrong side to remove wrinkles. Place velvet right side up on smooth, flat work surface. Using masking tape, tape selvage edges of velvet to work surface.

two Using masking tape, tape paper to stencil edges, extending size of stencil. Position stencil near center of fabric piece, then tape stencil extensions to outer edges of velvet. *Note: Tape applied to plush areas will remove pile when tape is pulled up.*

three Pour small amount of each paint onto palette. Using stencil brush and lt. green paint, dip brush into paint and brush off paint on fabric scrap until brush is nearly dry. Using a light, swirling motion, shade in leaf design beginning at outer stencil edges, working toward center of stencil. Using remaining stencil brush and leaf green paint, shade in some areas of stencil to add dimension. Allow to dry to the touch.

four Place and stencil portions of leaf stencil over remaining fabric, allowing to dry in between so paint does not smear. Use from one to four leaves at a time. Mask off stencil leaves with scraps of masking tape.

five Using iron, set paint by pressing wrong side of velvet.

Fabric Care: Dry clean.

Fabric embellished by Mary Jo Hiney

Geometric Blend—
—Theorem Painting

96

Materials:

Panne velvet fabric
Paint glazes: burgundy; deep sea green;
    plum; pumpkin; dk. purple

Basic Tools:

Artist's acetate
Circle template: 3"
Fabric marker
Iron and ironing board
Masking tape
Paint palette
Press cloth
Ruler
Stencil brushes: ¾" (5)
Utility knife

Instructions

one Using iron, press velvet on wrong side to remove wrinkles. Place velvet right side up on smooth, flat work surface. Using masking tape, tape selvage edges of velvet to work surface.

two Using marker, template, and utility knife, trace circle onto acetate and cut out for template. Using ruler, draw 5" square and cut out for template.

three Beginning at nearest corner, tape paper to stencil edges, extending size of stencil. Position stencil near center of fabric, then tape stencil extensions to outer edges of velvet. *Note: Tape*

applied to plush areas will remove pile when tape is pulled up.

four Pour small amount of each paint and glaze onto palette. Using stencil brush and pumpkin glaze, dab stencil brush on fabric scrap until brush is nearly dry. Using light, swirling motions, paint a 1¼-wide stripe across one outside edge.

five Using clean stencil brush and burgundy paint, dab second brush, following Step 4 and stencil 1¼"-stripe next to pumpkin stripe.

six Using clean brushes, and plum and deep sea green glazes, repeat Steps 4–5, filling stencil area with paint. Allow to dry to the touch. Remove template and tape.

seven Tape template to next position and repeat Steps 4–5 until desired number of squares have been painted.

eight Tape circle stencil onto the center of first painted square. Using clean brush and dk. purple glaze, paint circle, following Step 4. Paint remaining circles.

nine Allow paint to dry for 24 hours. Using iron and ironing board, press fabric with painted side down. Turn fabric with right side up and place press cloth over painted square and press to set paint. Press remaining squares.

Fabric Care: Hand wash in cold water and line dry.

Painted Velvet—

—Pigment on Burnout Velvet

Materials:
Burnout velvet: silk or silk rayon white
or off-white
Silk dye: 3—4 colors

Basic Tools:
Bamboo paintbrush
Mild soap
Spray/mist bottle with water
Stainless steel push pins
Wooden stretcher frame

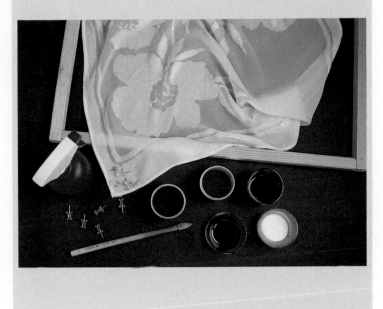

Instructions

one Wash velvet in mild soap
and rinse well. Allow to air dry.

two Using push pins, place fabric
on stretcher frame and secure. *Notes:
Fabric should be taut, but not tight.
Wooden stretcher frame can be made
from canvas stretcher bars purchased
at an art supply store.*

three Using spray bottle, mist
fabric and allow fabric to absorb
water. *Note: Fabric should not be
saturated.*

four Using paintbrush and silk
dyes, paint one color onto some of
the patterned areas of fabric. Rinse

brush and repeat with remaining colors, allowing
undyed areas of fabric between colors. After a few
minutes, colors will begin to blend together, filling
in undyed areas. Allow fabric colors to blend for
45 minutes.

five Repeat Step 4 until all fabric has been
painted. Allow fabric to dry 24 hours.

six Set dye, following manufacturer's
instructions.

Fabric Care: Launder as directed by fabric
manufacturer.

Variations:
▦ Instead of purchasing burnout velvet, create your
own design by following instructions for Velvet
Burnout on pages 121—122.
▦ Silk or silk rayon velvet without burnout may be
used in place of burnout velvet.

Sandra Clark has always been interested in art of the body and the ways the feminine form uses the body as canvas.

She became intrigued with fabric while living in Tokyo as a teenager. She was entranced with the aesthetics of everyday Japanese life and studied traditional Japanese art. She was most interested in the master dyers who created fabric paintings on silk for kimonos.

It was this interest that led Sandra to study textile arts. She holds a B.A. from Pennsylvania State University, M.A. from Northern Illinois University, and M.F.A. from the School of Art Institute in Chicago.

She creates fiber art wall pieces and wearable art working with dyes on linen and silk.

Sandra has taught and inspired college students in the arts. She recently retired and is currently spending the time working in her studio and participating in juried exhibitions. Her art is sold nationwide through galleries and museum shops.

Her work was recently exhibited in SOFA, Chicago, and the Museum of Contemporary Art, Chicago, as well as other fiber and painting exhibitions.

Traveling is one of Sandra's interests and her art reflects this. She looks for inspiration, fabrics, trims, beads, and unusual objects to be included in her work. She considers her art truly unique and one-of-a-kind with a global influence.

Sandra says of her work, "I want my fabric paintings to be an art form first, whether it is stretched on canvas or wearable."

Velvet Scarves
Painted and Embellished Velvet
Sandra Clark

Velvet Scarves
Painted Burnout Velvet
Sandra Clark

100

Fabric embellished by Roberta Glidden

Materials:

Crêpe de chine
Gutta resist
Silk dyes: assorted colors

Basic Tools:

Aluminum pie pan
Can: #303 (both ends cut out)
Canning pot
Charcoal pencil
Dish soap
Disposable plastic cups
Gutta applicator with metal tip
Heavy-duty aluminum foil
Heavy saucepan: 2 qt.
Masking tape
Newsprint paper
Old bath towel
Sponge brushes: one for each color
Stainless steel pushpins
Watercolor paintbrushes
Wooden stretcher frame

Painted Silk Vest
Roberta Glidden

Instructions:

one Using pushpins, place silk on stretcher frame and secure. *Note: Fabric should be taut, but not tight. Wooden stretcher frame can be made from canvas stretcher bars.* Using sponge brushes and silk paints that have been diluted to pastel colors, paint bull's eye design onto fabric. Allow paint to dry.

two Using charcoal pencil, lightly draw pattern on silk. Using gutta applicator, fill and apply gutta resist for design outline on background as desired. *Note: Turn fabric over and make certain that gutta penetrates through silk.*

three Mix four concentrated colors in separate plastic cups. *Note: Color may be used directly from bottle. Pour some of each color into separate clean plastic cups and add water to dilute color.*

four Using paint and sponge brushes, apply concentrated and diluted colors between resist lines as desired, allowing colors to blend on silk surface. Allow fabric to dry. *Note: Sponge brushes are used for large areas and paintbrushes are used for small areas.*

five Roll fabric in newsprint and using masking tape, tape bundle securely. See Steaming Fabric instructions on page 103. Steam fabric for one hour. Remove silk from steamer and unroll. Allow silk to cure for 12 hours.

six Dry clean silk to remove gutta. Using dish soap, handwash silk in warm water to remove unfixed dye. Rinse fabric until water runs clear.

Steaming Fabric:

Refer to Steaming Pan Diagram by Step numbers:

one Place 1" of water in canning pan.

two Place can in bottom of canning pan, and place pie pan on can. Place silk bundle on pie pan.

three Place an "umbrella" of aluminum foil over bundle to prevent steam from wetting silk. Bring water to a boil.

four Place old towel over top of canning pan to absorb steam.

five Place lid on canning pan. Place inverted saucepan on top of lid to retain heat.

Fabric Care: Hand wash and lay flat to dry.

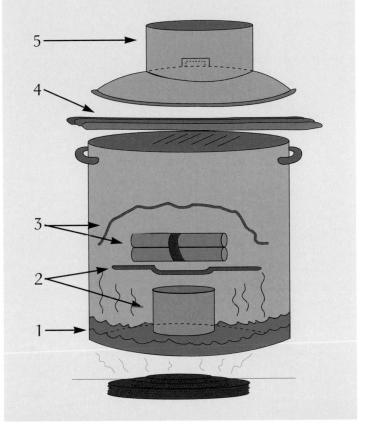

Steaming Pan Diagram

Silk Scarf
Silk Resist Painting
Roberta Glidden

Roberta Glidden does her silk painting in an 85-year-old bungalow in Ogden, Utah. The surrounding mountains, rivers, and canyons strongly influence her palette with subtle earth colors and the jewel tones of the summer flowers in her garden. She is also influenced by the energy and freedom found in children's art.

She developed an early interest in Asian art as a child taking lessons at the Seattle Art Museum. Later this interest was extended to historic textiles—particularly African—as she travelled to other continents.

Early on, Roberta experimented with cottons and rayons, but gravitated toward silk because of its sensual quality and the deeply saturated colors.

She has developed a line of silk scarves called Serape Line with the help of a seamstress and a marketing representative. Her Fall and Spring lines are distributed nationally.

Roberta received a B.A. from the University of Colorado. She has taught as an Artist in Education with the Utah Arts Council, University of Utah Textile Arts Program, 1991 Fall Semester at Sea with the University of Pittsburgh, and classes held in her studio.

She has designed two official scarves for the Salt Lake City Olympic Bid Committee. Her work has been published in *Volume II of Silk Painting for Fashion and Fine Art*, *The Best of Silk Painting*, and *The Complete Book of Scarves*. She illustrated the children's book *The Knee High Man* with her silk paintings.

Silk Jacket
Silk Resist Painting
Roberta Glidden

Silk Scarf
Silk Resist Painting
Roberta Glidden

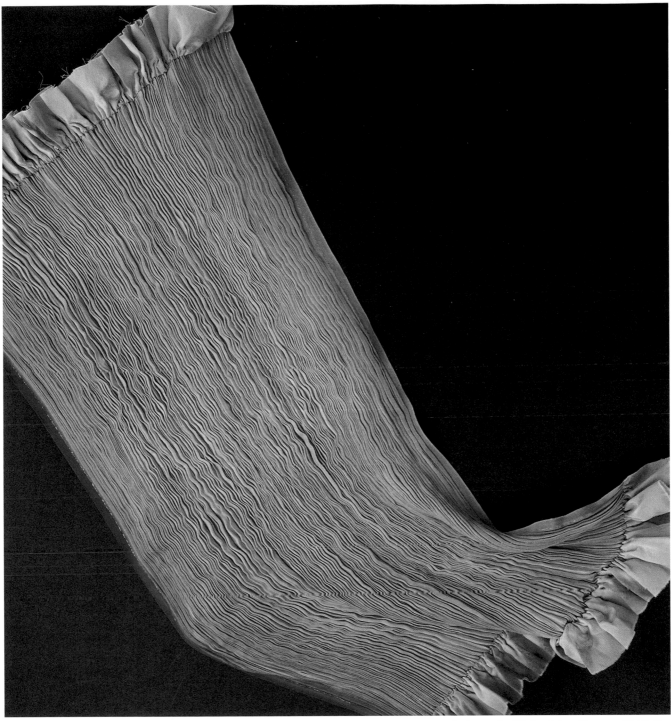

Fabric embellished by Karren K. Brito

Shibori—

—Color Discharge

This adaptation of a Japanese process uses discharge, which removes or changes the color of the fabric and makes a beautiful, pleated silk. When the silk is compressed, areas are created that resist, or in other words, areas are created where the color remover does not penetrate at all. Silk is the only fiber that can be discharged at home and retain semipermanent pleats. Medium and dark colors will give more color contrast when they are discharged. Black is the most difficult to discharge, but can also be the most rewarding.

The only way to determine if colored silk is dischargeable is to test it. There is not a specific brand or type of silk that can be consistently used without testing. Purchase a small piece of 100% silk or ask for a snippet from your fabric store.

One yard of 22"-wide fabric will yield approximately a 12" piece of fabric when the shibori process is complete. A 30" length of white plastic plumbing pipe will hold five to six yards of silk.

Materials:

Dischargeable crepe silk: 22"-wide, colored (minimum of 1 yd.)
Fabric color remover: (2–4 boxes) (must contain sodium hydrosulphite)
Sewing thread
White vinegar: 1 gal.

Basic Tools:

Dye pot: stainless steel or enamel, 5 qt. or larger
Fabric marker
Latex or waterproof apron
Latex or waterproof gloves
Plastic plumbing pipe: 6" inside diameter (30" length)
Plastic wash basin
Sewing machine
Small pitcher

Instructions

one Test piece of fabric to ensure that color will discharge. Place small amount of color remover powder in bowl and add several drops of hot water. Using toothpick, stir until powder is dissolved. Place mixture on silk and using hair dryer, heat solution. If color changes to lighter color, the color will discharge well. If color remains the same, the color is not dischargeable.

two Using straight pins, pin lengthwise edges of fabric together. Slide fabric over tube and pull on pinned edge until silk is snug against pipe. *Note: File or sand ends of pipe so that fabric will slide on without snagging.* Using fabric marker, mark where seam should be. Remove silk from pole. Using sewing machine, baste edges together, following marked seam.

three Slide silk onto pipe, keeping seam straight as shown in Diagram A. *Note: If fabric is not tight enough, then mark and sew second seam. Fabric should fit tightly, but should not be tight enough to tear fabric.*

Diagram A

four Scrunch fabric as compact as possible as shown in Diagram B. *Note: Wearing latex gloves will help keep a grip on the silk and aid in compacting fabric. One yard of silk should compress to approximately 6".* After all fabric has been compressed on pipe, rearrange fabric so creases are more uniform.

five Immerse pipe in water for 30 minutes. *Note: If silk is not soaked, the fabric will wick fabric remover and remove color from all areas of cloth.*

six Working in well-ventilated area, fill dye pot with one gallon of water and bring to a boil. Wearing apron and gloves, arrange pipe and wet silk in a plastic basin within reach of boiling water. Add box of color remover to boiling water.

seven Using small pitcher, quickly dip out solution and pour over silk as shown in Diagram C. Rotate pipe and continue to slowly pour boiling solution over silk until desired color is reached. If there is no significant color change, pour solution from basin back into dye pot and bring back to a boil. Add second box of color remover. Repeat pouring process until desired color or lightness is achieved. Up to four boxes of color remover may be used for discharge.

eight After desired shade is achieved, hand wash fabric (but do not remove from pipe) to remove solution odor. Rinse until odor is gone.

nine Clean color remover from dye pot, pitcher, and basin. Fill dye pot with vinegar, and bring to boil. Place fabric in basin, pour vinegar over fabric and pipe while slowly rotating pipe until all vinegar has been used.

ten Remove silk from basin and allow to dry completely. *Optional: Dry fabric using a fan. Note: Silk must be absolutely dry, avoid removing silk on a humid day.* Remove basting stitches and store lightly twisted.

Diagram B

Diagram C

Note: Pitcher and other utensils should be used only for discharge and dyeing purposes and not for culinary use.

Alternative Dyeing Options:

☐ Looser fit on pipe will produce larger pleats.

☐ Dyes or textile paints can be applied to fabric in place of color remover.

Remove cloth from pipe after discharge for unpleated pattern. Any type of cloth that will discharge, such as cotton, can be used for this technique.

Fabric Care: Dry clean, because pleats are semipermanent and will be lost if placed in water and washed.

Karren K. Brito produces a line of pleated silk shibori accessories through her company ENTWINEMENTS, which she founded in 1983.

She graduated with a B.S. in Chemistry from Bethany College in West Virginia. She completed her Ph.D. in Chemistry from the State University of New York at Buffalo.

Karen was a juror for the COE at Convergence '94. She was an exhibitor, panelist, and lecturer at Convergence '90. She has been published multiple times in *Ornament* and *Surface Design Journal*, as well as in *American Style, Color Trends, Distinction, Fiberarts, LOIMIEN LOMASSA*, and *Shuttle, Spindle and Dyepot*.

Her work has been exhibited and won awards throughout the United States and in Tokyo, Japan. Her works can be seen in the Philadelphia Museum of Art Shop, American Craft Museum Shop, Julia's Artisans in New York City, Norma May International in Charleston, Northern Possessions in Chicago, and Spirit of the Earth in Santa Fe. Karen belongs to a number of professional organizations.

Black Spectrum Shawl
Shibori
Karren K. Brito

Opera Shawl
Shibori
Karren K. Brito

Ribbon Shawl
Shibori
Karren K. Brito

Shawl
Shibori
Karren K. Brito

Shawl
Shibori
Karren K. Brito

Scarf
Shibori
Karren K. Brito

Photo Transfer—

—Photo Transfer and Appliqué

Photo transfer can be accomplished through two methods; heat and medium transfer. Both involve using color copies in place of original photos or art.

The following technique uses photocopy transfer medium, however, gallery pieces by artists who use the heat transfer method have been included.

Materials:

Fabrics:
    cotton: white
    cotton scraps: solid colors
Photocopy: color or black-and-white
    (5" x 7" or smaller)
Sewing thread

Basic Tools:

Circle template: 2"
Fabric glue
Household sponge
Paper towel
Photocopy transfer medium
Removable fabric marker: fine-point
Scissors:
    Craft
    Fabric
Sewing needle
Sponge brush: 1"
Waxed paper

Instructions

Photocopy Transfer:

one Using scissors, cut photocopy to edge of image. Place design right side up on waxed paper. *Note: When using lettering, make certain that lettering is mirror image for transfer.*

two Using photocopy medium and sponge brush, brush medium on photocopy approximately 1/16" or until image is no longer visible, but some color shows through. *Note: Follow manufacturer's instructions.*

three Place fabric right side up on smooth, flat work surface. Place photocopy and medium right side down on fabric. Place paper towel over photocopy and using photocopy medium bottle, lightly roll bottle over photocopy and fabric, smoothing out any wrinkles. Using fingers, press around photocopy edges.

four Clean any excess medium from fabric. Allow to dry 24–48 hours.

five Using wet sponge, saturate copy and allow to set for two minutes. Using damp sponge, rub off paper backing. Set aside for 30 minutes. Using damp sponge, firmly rub in circular motion to remove any remaining paper. Allow to dry 72 hours.

Fabric Buttons:

one Using circle template and fabric marker, draw circles on fabric scraps. Using fabric scissors, cut out circles.

two Using needle and thread, gather-stitch around edge of circle, slightly gather, and secure thread. Turn gathered edges under to center and glue to fabric. Allow to dry.

Fabric Care: Machine wash on gentle cycle in cool water. Machine dry on low.

MUMO began in Philadelphia in 1998 as a collaboration between artists Jennifer Schumow and Mary Smull. Their common interest of photography and textile lead them to integrate these mediums through the use of color photocopy heat transfer. They combine this technique with saturated print media color and collage in their surface design work.

Their works are presently available on floor-cloths, pillows, curtains, bags, and placemats. Their art can be seen in craft gallery shops around the United States.

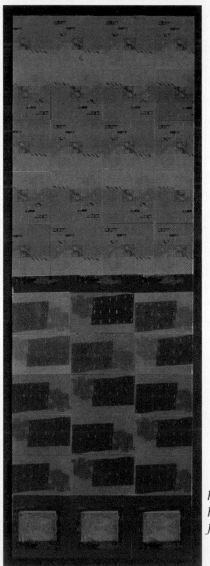

"Mars" (left) and "Pulp" (right) pillows
Heat Transfer
Jennifer Schumow and Mary Smull

Floorcloth
Heat Transfer
Jennifer Schumow and Mary Smull

Floorcloth
Heat Transfer
Jennifer Schumow and Mary Smull

Organza Curtains
Heat Transfer
Jennifer Schumow and Mary Smull

"Skyscrapers" (left) and "Bug" (right) Pillows
Heat Transfer
Jennifer Schumow and Mary Smull

Suzanne Evenson is a studio artist, photographer, teacher, and lecturer. She received her M.F.A. from Ohio State University and teaches Art and Art History at Columbus Community College.

Her work has been included in numerous juried and invitational exhibits in the United States, Australia, The Czech Republic, France, and Japan. Her work was included in Quilt International '95.

She has been featured in *Columbus Monthly*, *Fiberarts Design Book IV*, and *Fiberarts Design Book V*. She was a featured artist in the 1997 documentary, "Unraveling the Stories".

Her photography is incorporated into fabric pieces. Photographs, photograms, and scanned images are color copied and heat transferred onto fabric. Each piece is then further embellished by adding pieces of fabric, found objects, beads, machine- and hand-stitching.

There is a story behind each of Suzanne's works. She selects materials, allowing the interplay of color, pattern, and texture to guide her.

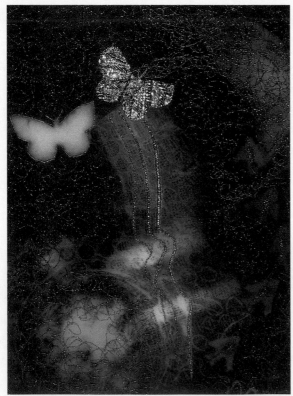

"Dreaming in the Garden IV"
Photogram
Suzanne Evenson

"Night Dancing II"
Photogram
Suzanne Evenson

114

Checkerboard Velvet—
—Embossed Velvet

Fabric embellished by Mary Jo Hiney

Materials:

Illustration board: 12½" x 25", white
Velvet fabric

Basic Tools:

Craft glue
Iron and ironing board
Pencil
Ruler
Spray/mist bottle with water
Straight pins
Utility knife

Instructions

one Using utility knife and ruler, cut illustration board in half widthwise, making two 12½" x 12½" square pieces. Using pencil, mark off one piece into 1¼" squares to make grid.

two Cut forty-one 1¼" squares from remaining piece. Using glue, adhere squares onto cardboard grid like a checkerboard pattern, leaving one grid square between cut-out squares as shown in Diagram A.

three Place illustration board face up on ironing board. Using pins, stretch and pin test piece of velvet right side down to ironing board.

four Using spray bottle, mist wrong side of velvet. Using iron set on medium heat, press iron on velvet, beginning at one end of checkerboard. Hold iron in place for five seconds. Lift iron straight up and move to next area, pressing iron for five seconds. Return to first section and press iron for five seconds. Press next section for five seconds. Repeat process and check

fabric to see if embossing is as desired. If not, continue to iron up to six times. Test will determine the number of times velvet will need to be pressed for embossing. Remove scrap fabric.

five Repeat Step 3 for setting up. Repeat Step 4 for embossing velvet, using test piece as time indicator.

Fabric Care: Dry clean.

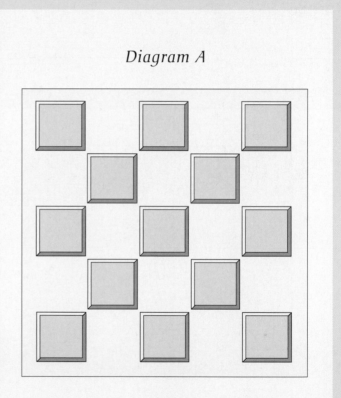

Diagram A

Fabric embellished by Mary Jo Hiney

Eclectic Embossed Velvet—
—Embossed Velvet

Materials that are found around the house can be combined together to emboss fabric, using an iron and ironing board. Fishnetting in two sizes and heavy lace were the embossing materials used for this model, along with rubber stamps.

Materials:
Krinkle velvet: rayon/acetate

Basic Tools:
Embossing materials
Iron and ironing board
Rubber stamps
Spray/mist bottle with water

Instructions

one Place embossing materials on ironing board surface, allowing edges to overlap. Place test piece of velvet right side down on materials.

two Using spray bottle, mist wrong side of velvet. Using iron set on medium heat, press iron onto velvet. Hold iron in place for five seconds. Lift iron straight up rather than sliding, and move to next area. Return to first section and press for five seconds. Repeat with second section. Continue to press until embossing is as desired. *Note: Test will determine the number of times velvet will need to be pressed for embossing. Remove scrap fabric.*

three Place velvet right side down over embossing materials. Repeat Step 2 for embossing velvet, using test piece as time indicator.

four Lift fabric and move to new section, rearranging embossing materials as desired on ironing board. Repeat Step 3, embossing remaining fabric. Remove embossing materials from ironing board.

five Determine areas for embossing with rubber stamp. Place rubber stamp, die side up, on ironing board. Place velvet right side down over stamp. Mist velvet on stamp location only. Press iron on velvet and stamp for 30 seconds, then lift iron straight up. Continue to emboss stamps onto velvet as desired.

Fabric Care: Dry clean.

Burnout Velvet Suit and Feather Handbag
Velvet Burnout and Dyed
Fabric designed by Jane Dunnewold
Suit made by Mary Jo Hiney

Silk Flower Burnout—

—Fabric Burnout

Fabric embellished by Mary Jo Hiney

Burnout is a technique that removes portions of fabric where a fabric remover has been applied and allowed to dry. Fabric remover compounds are made for specific fabric types, and in the case of the rayon/silk velvet blend, only the plush is removed, leaving the backing intact.

Materials:
Fabric remover
Velvet fabric (rayon/silk blend),
    light-colored

Basic Tools:
Masking tape
Newspaper

Instructions

one Enlarge Flower and Leaf Patterns 200% and photocopy.

two Place several layers of newspaper on work surface. Place design on newspaper and place velvet right side up, over design. *Notes: Use a light-colored fabric that allows design to be visible. Tape fabric edges to secure. Tape applied to plush areas will remove pile when tape is pulled up.*

three Shake fabric remover and apply thin layer, following design, wiping tip as necessary so remover does not spot or spill accidentally. Follow manufacturer's instructions if mistake or spill does occur. Move designs as desired and apply fabric remover. Allow to dry overnight.

four Machine dry velvet on low heat for 30 minutes to activate fabric remover or until design areas feel brittle. Rinse fabric in cold water, lightly rubbing design areas to remove rayon pile from silk backing. Allow fabric to dry.

Note: Always follow manufacturer's instructions.

Tips: Designs can be traced with marker on back side of pattern and used as a mirror image pattern if desired. Try using foam-core board and ½" straight pins to secure section of fabric if using a larger amount of yardage than can be taped to the work surface. Make certain fabric remover dries before moving on to a new section.

Fabric Care: Launder as directed by fabric manufacturer.

*Flower and Leaf Patterns
Enlarge 200%*

Diane Lewis is a stamp artist from Plano, Texas. She works in various mediums such as paper, fabric, and clay. Diane makes samples for product manufacturers and stamp companies. She also teaches stamping workshops.

Her articles and art have been featured in many publications including *Somerset Studio*, *RubberStampMadness*, *Rubber Stamper*, and *Stampington Book of Inspirations*. She is a featured artist in *Stampers Sampler* and the *Stamp Art Book* by Shrilyn Miller, and *The Art of Rubber Stamping* by Suze Weinberg. She is formerly a cover artist for *Rubber Stampin' Retailer*.

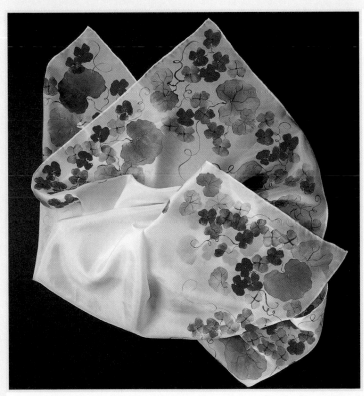

Geranium Scarf
Stamping on Silk
Diane W. Lewis

Floral Handbag
Stamping on Silk
Diane W. Lewis

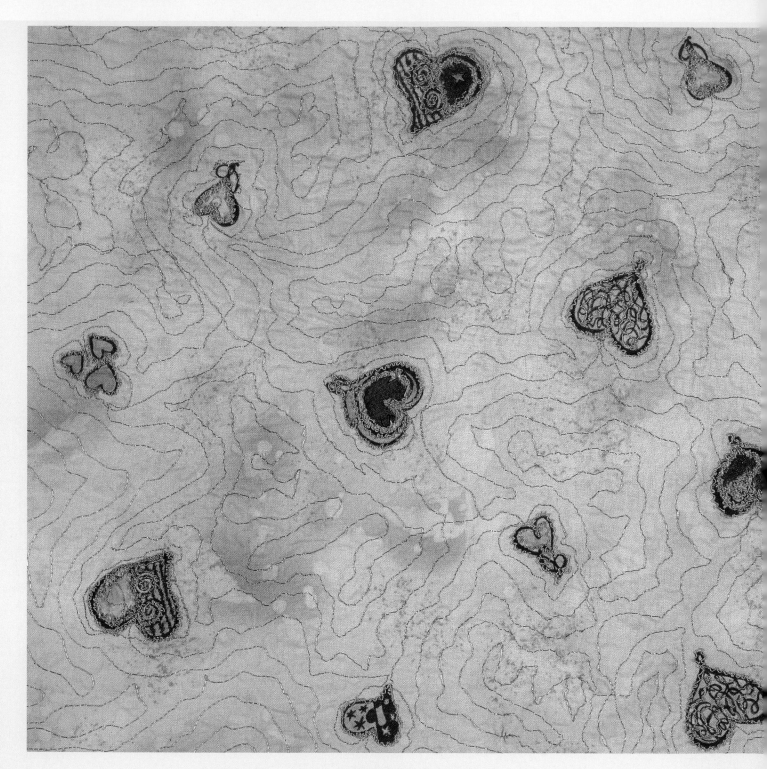

Stamped Hearts—
—Stamping, Fabric Burnout and Free-motion Stitching

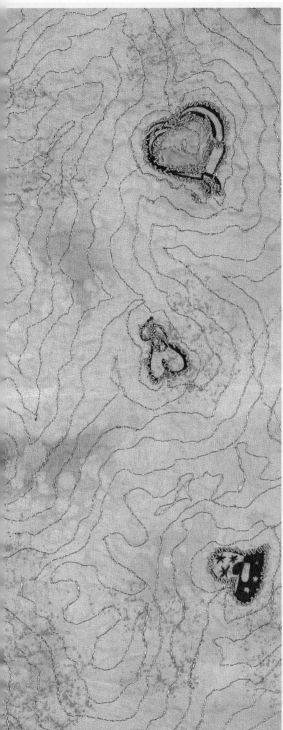

Floral Shawl
Stamping on Silk
Diane Lewis

Materials:

Fabric remover
Fabrics:
    Cotton print
    Cotton scraps: contrasting colors
    Muslin
Synthetic machine–embroidery threads:
    coordinating color; metallic

Basic Tools:

Fabric ink pad
Fabric marker: dual–tip, to match ink pad
Hair dryer
Rubber stamps: ¾"–2" (4–6)
Sewing machine with darning foot
Straight pins

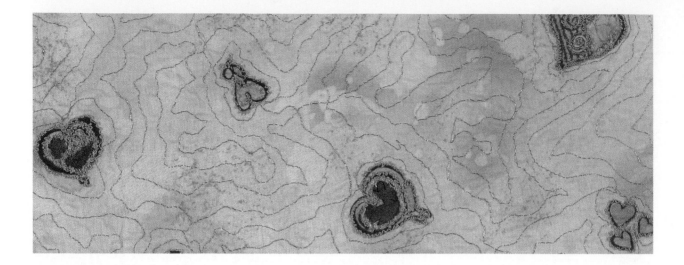

Instructions

one Using stamps and ink pad, randomly stamp designs onto right side of cotton print. Using fabric marker, outline and deepen details and color of stamped images. Using iron, press stamped images to set design.

two See Free-motion Stitching on page 18. Using sewing machine with darning foot and coordinating machine-embroidery thread, drop feed dogs and free-motion stitch narrow, wavy stitch around outside edge of stamped images.

three Free-motion stitch on inner section of stamped image. Leave inner section of several stamped images unstitched.

four Carefully fill center section of un-stitched stamped areas with fabric remover, following manufacturer's instructions. Use thin coat, making certain fabric remover does not extend past the outside edge of stitching. Using hair dryer, dry fabric remover, being careful not to scorch fabric.

five Rinse in cold water to remove treated fabric. Allow to dry.

six Place scraps of fabric behind open images. Repeat Step 2.

seven Place muslin on flat surface. Place stamped fabric right side up on muslin. Using straight pins, pin layers together.

eight Free-motion stitch with metallic machine-embroidery thread around all hearts and continue outward with rows of echo stitching spaced ¼"–⅜" apart. See above photo for echo stitch example.

nine Machine wash and dry fabric, to create a slightly puckered effect.

Note: See Velvet Burnout on pages 121–122 for additional information on burnout.

Fabric Care: Machine wash in warm water and machine dry.

Metric Equivalency Chart

mm-millimetres   cm-centimetres
inches to millimetres and centimetres

inches	mm	cm	inches	cm	inches	cm
⅛	3	0.3	9	22.9	30	76.2
¼	6	0.6	10	25.4	31	78.7
⅜	10	1.0	11	27.9	32	81.3
½	13	1.3	12	30.5	33	83.8
⅝	16	1.6	13	33.0	34	86.4
¾	19	1.9	14	35.6	35	88.9
⅞	22	2.2	15	38.1	36	91.4
1	25	2.5	16	40.6	37	94.0
1¼	32	3.2	17	43.2	38	96.5
1½	38	3.8	18	45.7	39	99.1
1¾	44	4.4	19	48.3	40	101.6
2	51	5.1	20	50.8	41	104.1
2½	64	6.4	21	53.3	42	106.7
3	76	7.6	22	55.9	43	109.2
3½	89	8.9	23	58.4	44	111.8
4	102	10.2	24	61.0	45	114.3
4½	114	11.4	25	63.5	46	116.8
5	127	12.7	26	66.0	47	119.4
6	152	15.2	27	68.6	48	121.9
7	178	17.8	28	71.1	49	124.5
8	203	20.3	29	73.7	50	127.0

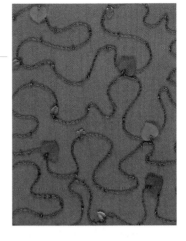

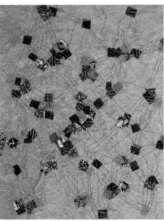

yards to metres

yards	metres	yards	metres	yards	metres	yards	metres	yards	metres
⅛	0.11	2⅛	1.94	4⅛	3.77	6⅛	5.60	8⅛	7.43
¼	0.23	2¼	2.06	4¼	3.89	6¼	5.72	8¼	7.54
⅜	0.34	2⅜	2.17	4⅜	4.00	6⅜	5.83	8⅜	7.66
½	0.46	2½	2.29	4½	4.11	6½	5.94	8½	7.77
⅝	0.57	2⅝	2.40	4⅝	4.23	6⅝	6.06	8⅝	7.89
¾	0.69	2¾	2.51	4¾	4.34	6¾	6.17	8¾	8.00
⅞	0.80	2⅞	2.63	4⅞	4.46	6⅞	6.29	8⅞	8.12
1	0.91	3	2.74	5	4.57	7	6.40	9	8.23
1⅛	1.03	3⅛	2.86	5⅛	4.69	7⅛	6.52	9⅛	8.34
1¼	1.14	3¼	2.97	5¼	4.80	7¼	6.63	9¼	8.46
1⅜	1.26	3⅜	3.09	5⅜	4.91	7⅜	6.74	9⅜	8.57
1½	1.37	3½	3.20	5½	5.03	7½	6.86	9½	8.69
1⅝	1.49	3⅝	3.31	5⅝	5.14	7⅝	6.97	9⅝	8.80
1¾	1.60	3¾	3.43	5¾	5.26	7¾	7.09	9¾	8.92
1⅞	1.71	3⅞	3.54	5⅞	5.37	7⅞	7.20	9⅞	9.03
2	1.83	4	3.66	6	5.49	8	7.32	10	9.14

Index